LEAD to WIN

HARSHIT BHAVSAR

UNIVERSAL HUNT®
www.universalhunt.com

Published by:
Unihunt Consulting Private Limited
405, Shukan Complex, Swastik Crossroad
Navrangpura, Ahmedabad-380009, Gujarat, India.
www.universalhunt.com
leadtowin@universalhunt.com
+91-79-40705000, 61908700, 66669600

LEAD TO WIN
ISBN: 978-81-8465-708-1

First Impression: 2011
Second Impression: 2011

Author's Note

LEAD to WIN is a launch pad to success, a platform that triggers a thought process and transcends a message that each person has an unidentified potential leader within him. Once discovered, leadership sets enormous limitless energy flowing, engulfing and positively influencing many lives around us. Once we learn to lead, we are bound to experience growth, satisfaction, achievement and success.

So in the process of evolving myself as a leader and in turn developing those around me also into leaders, I've embarked on the journey of writing this book. The journey of writing has run parallel with the journey of leadership experience. I am indeed grateful to all those who have believed in my vision and have become a part of Universal Hunt (www.universalhunt.com), contributing in creation of an inclusive vision and fulfilling many dreams of clients and candidates.

I would like to thank my family, colleagues, clients, associates, acquaintances, well-wishers, critics, friends, readers and many more whom I couldn't close in the box of relations, for making me what I am and contributing to the constant evolution of my persona.

I would like to thank you in advance for reading this book till the last line. Trust that you will savour the impact of content and quotes on daily basis. You may visit *www.universalhunt.com* for related products and services. Should you feel together we can make a difference, feel free to contact me on *harshit@universalhunt.com*

—Harshit Bhavsar

When you find a leader, follow;

When you identify a leader with in, LEAD

Contents

INTRODUCTION

The birth of my son Aditya became my life's defining moment. It gave me a fresh perspective about my life. Though clueless about how to react, sitting in a far away town at the time of my son's birth, I tried doing my bit. I shared the news with my friends, and went to shop in a newborns' store.

Again clueless about the needs of a newly born, I started wondering which items, toys, clothes, etc., to pick for him. Though, I bought a couple of things, but was not very sure if that would be of best use and interest to him.

Months went by, and I saw my boy transforming into a healthy baby brimming with a lot of energy and curiosity. I was surprised rather amazed to discover two fantastic qualities in an infant: "Lack of hesitation in getting involved with different people, i.e. his capacity to smile at everyone" and "high level of curiosity". These two very essential building blocks of success when seen in an infant left me spellbound. I saw him getting bored with materialistic things that I had brought for him. It perhaps then clicked me that I should provide him with a lifetime saviour, with a master key that would help him unlock doors of opportunities. Many parents must have thought of gifting their children something similar. Thereby, I feel most elated to gift and dedicate my son, my readers, and their children this book, which contains some key mantras of success and leadership. Assimilation of even a fraction of the total essence of this book would make my readers thrive in life with pleasure and sense of achievement.

Our character shapes our life and our life shapes our character.

Trust that *Lead to Win* becomes a priceless gift for your loved ones, your parents, friends, business partners, colleagues, team mates, and most importantly your children because your growth is directly proportional to the growth of people around you. It is always best to be in sync with each other, understand, and respect each other. This book shall surely be a medium to connect with people and show them that you care. It would certainly help in creating a better world around us.

Many a time we want to say so many things to our family members and to people working with us (our bosses, our colleagues, and our subordinates) in terms of what we think and what we want them to think on certain matters; express our ideology, and expect them to take advantage of what we feel will be fruitful. We all need this because we live and work interdependently, and the more there is synchronisation in broader understanding and respect towards each other the more this world becomes a beautiful place to live. Due to shortage of time we are not able to exchange and express ideas and thoughts in depth. I am sure this book will bring your thinking in alignment with each other creating groundwork for more matured understanding, and enhance tolerance for each other and build stronger relationships.

Hence I have penned down my thoughts, my learning, and my understanding about life, business, relations, and behaviour for best guidance to all my readers.

This book attempts to dissect leadership and its importance in living a successful life with feeling of satisfaction, growth, and achievement. There is a message for formation of noble character that would make one's life worth all the effort.

Introduction

Right from our birth till our death we undergo continuous process of evolution. People who evolve themselves maximally in the course of life emerge as leaders whom others try to follow.

Life is a process of defining the purpose of living and then finding means of executing the same, and in the process, improving on the purpose, at times redefining purpose as well as means of achieving the same. What is important in the entire process is relishing this sequence, elevating the benchmark, evolving as humans, until we feel thoroughly successful and satisfied.

Our character shapes our life and our life shapes our character. People with noble characters, purpose, and meaningful life are leaders in true sense of the word. Tremendous satisfaction is the fruit of successful leadership.

Many a time we hear that leaders are born and never made. This is normally believed by people who never aspire to be leaders. We all have a leader within us, which is a combination of characters coming out in several degrees or proportion under certain situations. Leaders aren't born, they are made. And they are made just like anything else, through hard work. And that's the price we'll have to pay to achieve our goal.

So, I wish you all have an evolving time as you go through this book! Let this be a transformative medium for you, may you all be leaders and taste success in its utmost capacity.

WHO SHOULD READ THIS BOOK?

If you are asking a question "Is this book for me?", then I would say that the very fact you are holding this book explains your need for it. I would say, "Of course! It is for you!" The very fact that the word "leadership" fascinated you to pick this book up for reading indicates your desire to be a go-getter and a leader. Your desire to develop leadership traits and thereby lead a better life subconsciously or consciously pulled you towards this book and glued you till this very line that you are reading.

This book is meant for all those who desire to experience a successful life by leading. There is a leader within all of us and this book will bring forth a better understanding of leadership traits and help each of us in awakening the leader within us.

"The test of leadership is not to put greatness into humanity, but to elicit it, for the greatness is already there."

—*James Buchanan*

It will help you become a better human being, a successful corporate, political, religious or social leader. It would guide you to behave and succeed like a leader at every stage, age and situation in life.

Lead to Win is highly recommended for every parent who wishes to impart best lessons of growth to their children and guide them in developing best characters. It will help the parents in carefully shaping the future of their children instilling in them courage, conviction and determination to become successful human beings.

The book will specially appeal to youngsters. As character traits develop and strengthen in young age, this handbook will guide the youth in carefully analysing and developing their leadership traits to ultimately make them achievers in life.

This handbook is for sure to act as a guide to develop multiple traits which when used together in different situations and proportions would infuse the power of leadership. Being a leader will not only help us in leading a successful life but it'll also help us in improving the life of others around us creating a better environment for all.

The piece of work is most helpful for decision makers for recruiting right leaders for their institutions/organisations who can lead their empires in the right direction benefiting the stakeholders, and hence the economy as a whole. I am sure that once you finish reading this book, it would change your perception about yourself and about those who come in your contact. You would have a better understanding of people as a result.

For clear and easy understanding of leadership traits, *Lead to Win* contains several examples of world leaders hailing from different backgrounds and streams. In order to give a deeper insight into the lives and leadership traits of world famous figures, I have penned down accounts of their life. You may have dinner with Nelson Mandela, lunch with Gandhi, and coffee with Alexander.

> *Leadership is something you can't touch, you can't feel, it is not tangible; but you most certainly recognise it when you see it.*

Reading about each leader would be highly inspiring. I assure that these instances would ignite in my readers a will to accomplish any task under the sun.

It should not be expected that a person will be a national hero or an international level business person or a global religious leader in a go. But growth always begins with small acts of leadership under different situations. Every small act of leadership would give a feeling of satisfaction, achievement and growth. Such small acts would pile up to give larger success. Once nurtured that as a habit, then growth and success would become a way of living.

HOW TO USE THIS BOOK?

Now, I would like to elaborate on how this book is designed in terms of its content and how it can benefit the reader.

Content primarily is divided into three parts.

It gives detailed understanding of each trait of leadership, which once put together in different proportion transforms an individual into a leader. After reading the book completely for once, it would not be a bad idea to read and ponder over one trait every morning soon after you wake up. Allow yourself some time to reflect within. Reading another trait at night before you go to sleep would add impetus to your evolving thought process.

Most of the traits are explained using examples of world leaders which are in form of their mini biographies. This is not the end; it just sets the ball rolling. Literature shapes our thoughts, so this has been designed to help readers cultivate a habit of reading biographies of leading personalities. Decide a schedule and plan to read. What you would learn from this would be priceless and life transforming.

Every section is studded with quotes on leadership. The quotes basically substantiate our understanding of the associated section of the book. This would act to facilitate strong thoughts and create positive energy around you. If one thought can make one of your days progressive, I am sure many such good thoughts can change your life. These pearls of wisdom will help you look at life with healthy perspective. Keep the book before you every minute, on your desk, at an accessible place so that you can gain confidence for moving up in life. Whenever you have spare time, like during a coffee break, or in between a meeting, or after writing a lengthy email, just grab this book, read a few quotes, and rejuvenate your thoughts. A collection of several actions packed, energising, thought provoking, stimulating quotes alone is worth the dive into this book.

Skip a few Sunday movies and spend time at home or farm house or hotel with your kids, and read this book with them. Discuss the quotes. Try finding out more information about leaders even beyond what is mentioned in this book. Read their biographies and books written by them. I assure that you would undergo a beautiful experience. Have a habit of discussing books on dining table and see the change!

WHY PEOPLE WANT TO BECOME LEADERS?

At the end of your life you would either say, "I wish I would have," or "I'm glad I did". What you say would depend on whether you have lived the life of a follower or a leader.

Either you will control your own destiny or someone else will control it for you.

Before we understand traits of leadership, we should first understand why we want to become a leader. The answer lies in a much larger question, which is "what is the purpose of life?" Leaders possess a strong "sense of purpose" in life, strong enough to relentlessly carry out tasks in the pursuit of achieving the same.

We want SATISFACTION & FULFILMENT in life.

It is derived from SUSTAINABLE GROWTH.

It is experienced as a result of continuous achievement.

This demands a big, crystal clear VISION, which should be your Purpose of Life.

To fulfil a large vision you need more people whose smaller dreams are captured in your vision.

This is the process of being a LEADER.

It is a basic human nature to desire more. We all long to derive satisfaction and pleasure from whatever activities we carry out throughout our life. Each activity is guided by a purpose or a goal, which is based on the expected satisfaction or pleasure one would derive on fulfilment of that goal.

Life shrinks or expands in proportion to one's courage.

Once successful, once the goal is achieved, we desire to move on to a higher level of satisfaction. This elevates the standard of purpose, implying that we want to set a higher goal or benchmark that would involve more challenges and higher level of activity to break monotony. This way we keep expanding our horizons by challenging our limits and discovering our strengths as well as overcoming weaknesses. It is the process of continuous growth and evolution. In this process, in order to achieve material, intellectual, social, emotional, and spiritual growth, we need to execute a variety of things that are of larger interest. This is process of "expansion of horizons".

Leadership is about listening to others and valuing their opinions.

When we get set on expanding our horizons, we need to go beyond our individual capacities. We need more people to achieve more tasks and bigger goals.

You should have a concrete reason behind your purpose.

Leadership is a challenge to become something more than average.

There should be clarity regarding why others should participate in your goal when they all have freedom to define their separate individual goals for their personal happiness and satisfaction.

In order to ensure that others accept your goal and merge their individual goals with yours, the nature and scale of your goal has to be all-encompassing, providing every follower with a common vision, which would attract them to join the group, institution or organisation led by you.

Hence a person with very strong sense of purpose and large vision would always require people with equally strong capacity to execute series of tasks leading to fulfilment of the greater vision. One needs to learn the art of leading people to achieve the larger vision encompassing multiple smaller goals.

LEADERSHIP – CHARACTER FORMATION

Becoming a leader is being you; it is that simple, and hence that difficult.

The process of development of character ultimately shapes our life, influencing our way of life and the degree of satisfaction we derive out of it.

Process of Character Formation

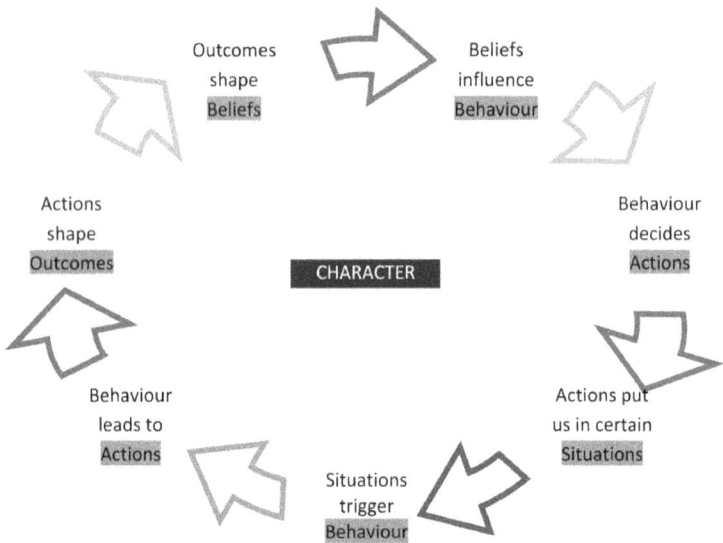

Outcomes shape **Beliefs**

Beliefs influence **Behaviour**

Actions shape **Outcomes**

CHARACTER

Behaviour decides **Actions**

Behaviour leads to **Actions**

Situations trigger **Behaviour**

Actions put us in certain **Situations**

During our journey of life, we find ourselves in different situations arising out of our actions and natural circumstances.

In every situation, we behave in a certain fashion with an expectation of certain preconceived outcomes; these expectations of outcomes are normally based on our past experiences under similar situations. Depending on the outcomes of our behaviour, which may be expected, or unexpected, good or bad, comfortable or disturbing, we tend to define success and failure.

This success or failure further sharpens our understanding of outcomes in context to our behaviour and situation, and we try to repeat or change our behaviour based on our perception of outcome, till we achieve a desired result or change our expectations of outcomes. It means once we achieve an outcome, for the next time, we would either repeat our actions, or change our actions and expectations.

All these events and our reactions to them shape us for future events and develop certain traits or characteristics within us over a period of time. We all have these traits in different proportions depending on the situations we have gone through and the ways we have reacted to them.

We consciously want to develop certain traits that would help us achieve desired results under certain circumstances.

During the process of evolution, we develop characteristics based on experiences and situations we have gone through or seen or heard someone else going through. We sometimes like to put ourselves into certain situations "knowingly" with the expectation of developing certain character traits so that we undergo improvement in our personality. This helps us achieve desired results in future while we face similar situations "unknowingly or accidently". We all do this in order to obtain a sense of achievement.

Leadership is a combination of multiple traits developed over a period of time. We all have leadership traits lying dormant within us. These awaken and get developed in different proportions under different situations.

This book attempts to highlight that we all have a leader within us and we all can develop and grow leadership traits by carefully analysing situations in which various people have displayed these traits.

Traits, situations, and events highlighted in this book are not the ultimate. However, after reading this they would help you think in a sharper and a smarter way. They would change the way you start looking at the world and at the opportunities available in the world to lead a better life.

We will first try to highlight WHAT are the character traits of a leader, WHY one desires the need to develop such traits and HOW one should develop them.

A person's observable behaviour reflects his character. One's behaviour can be strong or weak, good, or bad. A person with a strong character shows drive, energy, determination, self-discipline, and willpower. He visualises what he wants and peruses it relentlessly until he achieves it. He attracts people by his aura of leadership. On the other hand, a person with a weak character shows none of these traits. He does not know what he wants, is unfocussed and clueless, and is often driven by others. He lacks discipline, is disorganised, and vacillates in his decisions and opinions. As a result, he does not attract followers.

Lead to Win attempts to simplify leadership under different situations. It could be business leadership, political leadership, religious leadership or social leadership and more. So in whichever field you might be, this book will help you in attaining leadership there and then.

Leaders define excellence through good character. Pursuing excellence and task accomplishment are two independent things.

Character develops over time. Many think that much of a person's character is formed early in life. However, it cannot be known exactly how early in life one's character develops. But, it is safe to claim that character does not change quickly.

Organisations, institutions, and nations are built by leaders with strong and good characteristics, people who guide others to the future and can be trusted and relied upon. To be an effective leader, your followers must trust you and follow your vision. This behaviour wins loyalty, and ensures your organisation's continuity and growth. Trust in a leader is built by display of good character traits displayed by his noble beliefs, values, and superior skills. In short, leadership comprises multiple small traits or characteristics made up of

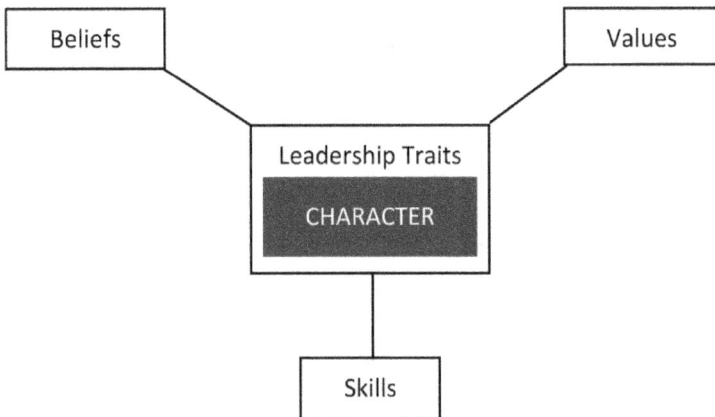

```
┌──────────┐                        ┌──────────┐
│ Beliefs  │                        │  Values  │
└────┬─────┘                        └────┬─────┘
     │                                   │
     └──────────┐         ┌──────────────┘
            ┌───┴─────────┴───┐
            │ Leadership Traits│
            │ ┌──────────────┐ │
            │ │  CHARACTER   │ │
            │ └──────────────┘ │
            └────────┬─────────┘
                     │
               ┌─────┴─────┐
               │   Skills  │
               └───────────┘
```

beliefs, values, and skills.

Belief is nothing but reflection of the knowledge we possess. It is the simplest form of mental representation, and therefore, one of the building blocks of conscious thoughts. Beliefs are rooted deeply within us. They could be assumptions or convictions we hold true regarding people, human nature, concepts, or things like life, death, religion, what is good, what is bad, etc.

Values are an integral part of every person and culture. Values are important as they influence a person's behaviour to weigh the importance of alternatives. To understand people, it is imperative to understand their values, beliefs, and assumptions that motivate their behaviour. Values build personal identity and bring sense of worth in a person. They are indicative of what is beneficial, important, beautiful, desirable, constructive, etc. Values help people solve common human problems and ensure a healthy survival. However, at times, values can be negative and destructive. One should decline nurturing negative values for they can never help a person in becoming a leader.

Success is not an accident but it is a skill that can be learnt by leadership.

Skills are the expertise in knowledge and creative abilities that a person acquires throughout life. These are learned capacity to carry out pre-determined results often with the minimum outlay of time, energy, or both. The ability to learn a new skill varies for every individual. Some skills come almost naturally, while others come only by complete devotion, study, and practise.

Now, after having discussed the three prime parameters of character we would concentrate on understanding essential traits, which result in the formation of a leader. A leader by virtue of such character traits is recognised by others who trust him and follow him in the process of achieving his vision, the purpose of life, which is of course of larger interest for all involved.

LEADERSHIP TRAITS

This book highlights certain intrinsic or fundamental traits of leadership which are often missed out by analysts, thinkers and philosophers in the process of concentrating on apparently obvious and easily recognizable traits. Many a time what has been interpreted as traits of leadership are actually the outcome of a few finer elementary traits.

Furthermore, we will analyse the very core of each of these basic traits, which result in the development of subsequent traits and formation of overall leadership character which is a collective outcome of these traits or characteristics. These traits are observed to be present in various proportions whenever leadership behaviour is displayed by a person.

Leaders are followed by masses. However, in some cases due to one wrong move or development of some negative trait a leader has a risk of becoming unpopular. He might lose trust of his followers and lose his charm as a leader. There are some people who are not leaders per se but display very strong leadership characters under a certain situation for certain period of time. But their spirit fizzles out with time.

DISCIPLINE results in creation of SUSTAINED LEADERSHIP character, which when developed at a fast rate transform leaders into legends. Such people survive far beyond their life and are remembered and honoured in future. Even when they don't live, they attract fans and followers through their ideology and principles.

Possessing traits is not enough. It is important to exhibit qualities so that they come to people's notice. As seeing is believing, so people would accept leaders only when their visible traits are captivating. It isn't enough to be neutral. For example, just because you are not dishonest, people will not

> *It's not important that you know that you have knowledge, it's important that you show that you have knowledge.*

recognise your honesty until or unless you display this trait through your actions. Displaying competence would inspire people to have faith and confidence in you. Leaders have tremendous capacity to learn and then demonstrate effectively what they have learnt.

ENVISIONING

Some people see things; and say "Why?"
But some dream things that never were and say "Why not?"

Vision is something that doesn't allow you to sleep and yet keep you energised next morning. It makes you fall in love with yourself and life in general.

What is the purpose of your life? What do you want to do in life?

Take a piece of plain paper and write as elaborately as you can, in response to this thought, before you move ahead.

This is a vital question that you must ask yourself. Surprisingly enough, most of us do not even bring this thought in mind till the end of our life. Many are not even clear about what to do tomorrow if they are alive. We are simply involved into monotony of life and get driven by life's circumstances instead of shaping our life. Once you find an answer to this, life would be full of passion.

Every one of us during our stay on this earth indulges into some or the other activity. Envisioning is nothing but being aware of "WHAT to do?" It means identifying the purpose of life. It sets the ball rolling. Many times we are simply caught in executing what others have decided to do, losing track of our own goals. The sooner we realise what we want to do, the better it is. One thing which is important to understand is leaders are not born with vision. Vision formation occurs based on our experiences. Sometimes it happens at an early stage, sometimes it happens late, and sometimes it doesn't happen at all!

Based on the quality and size of vision, a desire sets in, which helps us to achieve this vision that defines our purpose of life. The intensity or passion for this purpose is decided by the vision. The intensity and passion further shape our thoughts and beliefs which give way to our actions. Process of execution of actions develops skills. Outcomes of actions and alignment of that with expectations further stimulates our thoughts and convictions, strengthening them or weakening them depending on the intensity of desire triggered by quality and size of vision/purpose.

This cyclic process gives birth to traits that shape our character, which determines the quality of life, amount of growth, quantum of feeling of fulfilment, and sense of achievement.

Envisioning is the art and science of anticipating and participating in creation of future.

Alexander the Great had envisioned "one world, one people". He had the vision to expand his empire at a very young age and wanted to unite the whole world under his rule. During his lifetime he conquered the then-known world. He controlled Greece, captured Persia and Egypt where he also built a city. He became the king of Macedonia and a pharaoh in Egypt. Mahatma Gandhi envisioned independent and united India. Martin Luther King Jr. envisioned America with equal rights for all. Nelson Mandela envisioned delivering his people in South Africa from bondage of apartheid.

"Leadership should be born out of the understanding of the needs of those who would be affected by it."

—Marian Anderson

"All of the great leaders have had one characteristic in common: it was the willingness to confront unequivocally the major anxiety of their people in their time. This, and not much else, is the essence of leadership."

—John Kenneth Galbraith

"The cardinal responsibility of leadership is to identify the dominant contradiction at each point of the historical process and to work out a central line to resolve it."

—Mao Tse-Tung

It would be interesting to think what made these people envision their future beforehand. We should try to understand what goes behind the mind of a leader that enables him of such perfect envisioning?

I personally feel that envisioning is one of the most important traits that reveal a leader's sharpness of mind. Every leader has developed an inherent power of envisioning situations. Envisioning is primarily combination of three things which happen simultaneously and not necessarily in sequential order:

- Understanding the larger picture

- Opportunity identification

- Creation of successful execution plan

Understanding the larger picture:

We have a lot of information flowing around us in form of various mediums of communication. Problem is that most of the people are unable to understand and interpret the information.

Success is the gap b e t w e e n information and interpretation.

There are some people who though interpret the information but are not able to integrate or derive any pattern or meaning out of that. Leaders have the capacity to capture the information, understand it in the simplest of its form, discard unwanted information, interlink the relevant information where required, and develop a larger picture, synthesising every information

A leader is interested in finding the best way, not his own way.

possible which makes sense.

Overall larger picture that a leader can visualise, which is derived out of the information available, is beyond the capacity of normal people. This is primarily because of their habit of seeing life from a different and more importantly larger perspective. They can gather, digest, and assimilate most important information in a short span of time with absolute speed and clarity, and create a sense out of that.

Opportunity identification:

"Men make history, and not the other way around. In periods where there is no leadership, society stands still. Progress occurs when courageous, skilful leaders seize the opportunity to change things for the better."

—Harry Truman

After a situation is completely analysed and a larger view is understood, leaders have the ability to spot opportunities which can fulfil larger purpose of life. Whether a person is a business leader or a political leader or a social leader, he should be able to identify the opportunity in the interest of his larger goal and provide benefit to larger group of people.

Creating action plan:

Having understood the purpose in the form of an opportunity

Thin line between dream and vision is EXECUTION.

available in his personal and larger public interest, leader has the capacity to breakdown the vision into smaller goals, identify action required to achieve each goal, break down each action into smaller tasks and identify parameters to monitor as well as evaluate the progress of the task execution. He then breaks down the larger picture into smaller views which can be understood by the common men who would take responsibility for executing this. He is also good at designing systems and processes, and monitors them in the best possible manner. Based on his understanding, a leader is successfully able to explain and convince others about his perception of future events and their likely outcomes. A leader can understand the skill sets and identify people who would execute these tasks successfully with those skill sets.

All in all leaders are great visionaries with ability to understand larger picture and perceive the events as well as their future outcomes based on the understanding and synthesis of present and past events and their outcomes.

Every person undergoes a turbulence of ideas, thoughts, and conviction before vision formation takes place. Sooner the better, though there is no definite time when a person finds the purpose to adhere to passionately, where he puts all his resources to accomplish that purpose. At the time of formation of vision there would be multiple thoughts from various perspectives coming in the mind of a leader.

While envisioning, it is most important to keep your ideas to yourself, until they are well formulated and take a concrete shape, which is powerful enough to develop same level of conviction in others. Otherwise you would end up confusing people around you. Vision should signify the clarity of purpose and at the same time should be strong and large enough to inspire people and infuse passion in them.

"Slump, and the world slumps with you. Push, and you push alone."

—*Laurence Peter*

Leaders need to be distinct from others and this distinction comes from carrying out responsibility that no ordinary people can carry out. One needs to learn to remain aloof for some time, to do proper justice to the formation of vision otherwise one would share his ideas to all not knowing which one would work in the direction of achievement of purpose. All those who like the idea would jump to work on it and those who don't, would start working against it. People would go back and forth when the idea may not even come about at all. A leader must be able to identify between idea and vision.

"A leader takes people where they want to go. A great leader takes people where they don't necessarily want to go, but ought to be."

—*Rosalynn Carter*

Apart from developing a clear vision, a leader must be capable of conveying the same lucidly. Leaders not only have a clear idea of what is possible, they practically prove it. They understand where they want to lead their people, keep a definite plan to get them there, along with having the ability to communicate the destination to people. Mahatma Gandhi, Nelson Mandela, and Alexander the Great best reflected the characteristic of envisioning.

Mahatma Gandhi:

Be the change you want to see in the world.

Mohandas Karamchand Gandhi was the pre-eminent political and spiritual leader of India during the Indian independence movement. When India was bound in the shackles of British Empire and colonialism was at its peak, Gandhi had envisioned independent and united India and made this vision the purpose of his life. He had always kept a larger picture in mind. His each move, each action was directed towards achieving this goal, which he achieved through non-violence. He was the pioneer of *satyagraha*—resistance to tyranny through mass civil disobedience, a philosophy based on *"ahimsa"* or total non-violence—which led India to independence and inspired movements for civil rights and freedom across the world. He is officially honoured in India as the Father of the Nation; his birthday, 2 October, is commemorated as the International Day of Non-Violence.

Let's understand the important events of his life to get a clear insight in to the thought process and actions of a visionary.

Nobody can hurt me without my permission.

Gandhi's foremost employment of "non-violent civil disobedience" happened while he was an expatriate lawyer in South Africa, during the resident Indian community's struggle for civil rights. Non-violence and non-cooperation were the most effective tools he discovered to express his reservations against any powerful system. After his return to India in

Whenever you are confronted with an opponent, conquer him with love.

1915, he organised several protests by peasants, farmers, and urban labourers against excessive land-tax and discrimination; again under strict adherence to non-violence. After 1921, when he became the leader of Indian National Congress, Gandhi led nationwide campaigns to ease poverty, expand women's rights, build religious and ethnic amity, end *untouchability*, and increase economic self-reliance. Above all, he aimed to achieve *"Swaraj"* (self-rule) in India. These activities were carried out binding the whole nation towards a common purpose, which was the independence. Gandhi led thousands of followers in the Non-cooperation movement that protested the British-imposed salt tax with the 400 km "Dandi Salt March" in 1930. Later, in 1942, he launched the "Quit India" movement demanding immediate independence for India. Gandhi spent a number of years in jail in South Africa as well as in India. He organised events symbolic of non-cooperation and non-violently protested against injustice until he successfully bound the whole nation to create a common voice demanding independence.

As a practitioner of non-violence, he swore to speak the truth and led a very modest and simple life. He wore simple clothes woven with hand-spun yarn. His dressing style was symbolic of non dependence on imported items. He ate simple vegetarian food, and also undertook long fasts for self-purification and social protest. Mahatma Gandhi in true sense recognised the value of religious tolerance and sovereignty for the people of India, he used his life to make it possible.

Gandhi adopted all possible means to instigate the changes he was seeking: his diet, his clothing, his community, his speech. Gandhi always said, "My life is my message".

Gandhi not only crafted a vision of independent India or identified means to achieve the same through non-violence, disobedience, and self reliance but also actively adopted these principles in every move of his life making millions of people follow him and participate in his vision, making it a reality.

Nelson Mandela:

Nelson Mandela born on 18 July 1918, served as President of South Africa from 1994 to 1999. He was the first South African president to be elected in a fully representative democratic election. Nelson Mandela's vision was about the "Universal Declaration of Human Rights and entitlement of each person to these rights".

"It is better to lead from behind and to put others in front, especially when you celebrate victory when nice things occur. You take the front line when there is danger. Then people will appreciate your leadership."

Before his presidency, Mandela was an anti-apartheid activist, and the leader of "Umkhonto we Sizwe", the armed wing of the African National Congress (ANC) that had its main objective to end apartheid and create a multi-racial South Africa. Nelson Mandela made the ANC vision as his own. In retaliation to the new apartheid policies, the ANC Youth League drafted Program of Action calling for mass strikes, boycotts, protests, and passive, resistance. These were sincerely implemented and the organisation acquired more activists.

In 1962, he was arrested and convicted of sabotage and other charges, and was sentenced to life imprisonment. Mandela served twenty-seven years in prison, mostly on Robben Island during which he grew more politically active in South Africa. Mandela clearly held a positive vision of a racially harmonious South Africa during these years in jail and helped bring it into reality by communicating his vision through his wife, Winnie Mandela, and the people who were able to gain access to him and bring out word.

He became a political icon and the world associated South

Africa's freedom with his freedom. On his release from prison, South Africans faced a new challenge of creating a multi-racial society and getting rid of malice of the past. Mandela took the onus of this new challenge on his shoulder and managed to put a new vision into the hearts of the South African people. "Revenge would not bring South Africa the much longed for prosperity", he often said. He encouraged the Black South African people to reconcile with the White South Africa, and let go of the past. He has always encouraged the people of South Africa to learn about each other, to compromise and create a South Africa where race and colour did not matter. Following his release from prison on 11 February 1990, Mandela led his party in the negotiations that led to multi-racial democracy in 1994. As president from 1994 to 1999, he gave priority to reconciliation. This was the birth of a Rainbow Nation.

Although people associate Nelson Mandela with the liberation struggle of South Africa, his message is more than that. It is about the Universal Declaration of Human Rights and about the need for entitlement of these rights to all people.

According to Mandela, "the values of happiness, justice, human dignity, peace, and prosperity have a universal application because each community of people and every individual are entitled to them". Similarly, he feels that no person can truly say he is blessed with happiness, peace, and prosperity when others continue to be afflicted with misery, armed conflict, terrorism and deprivation. Once he accomplished this goal in South Africa, Nelson Mandela continued to pursue ways and means to help other communities access these rights.

Mandela has received more than 250 awards over four decades, most notably the 1993 Nobel Peace Prize.

Alexander the Great:

Alexander III of Macedon (356–323 BC), popularly known as Alexander the Great, was a Greek king of Macedon. He is

Circumstances? What Circumstances? I create Circumstances!

well known for the creation of one of the largest empires in ancient times. He was born in Pella and was trained under the great philosopher Aristotle.

Alexander's vision was to unite the then known world under one ruler. He believed that by inter-marrying the various races, and blending best of each

Heaven cannot brook two suns, nor earth two masters.

culture, one would eventually create one race; what he called as "one world, one people".

Alexander is one of the greatest generals in history of this world. Whenever he conquered any new state, he was modest enough to honour their soldiers and commanders who had died in battle. He merged soldiers of

I had rather excel others in the knowledge of what is excellent, than in the extent of my power and dominion.

the opponents with his army to form a greater army ensuring equal treatment to conquered people. He fought hard and suffered along with his soldiers at war. If they didn't have water or food, he would not accept food or drink either. When the soldiers would walk, he also walked and refused to ride or be carried. He

Remember, upon the conduct of each depends the fate of all.

was a leader by example for his troops.

There is nothing impossible for him who will try.

Even though his empire collapsed after his death, his dream continued to live on. Today, the vision of Alexander "one world, one people" has emerged in what is known as the European Union with its borders stretching from Portugal in the west, to Sweden in the north, Cyprus in the south, Ukraine, and Turkey in the east. This zone is a region of mixed cultures and diverse racial groups. But Alexander took only thirteen years to unite the world (from his twenty years of age till his thirty-three years of age after which he died in Babylon in 323 BC), whereas unity of Europe is still an ongoing process, the continent is still evolving to stand as a single entity. It is difficult to imagine someone conquer almost the whole world by the age of thirty-two. This signifies nothing but very clear vision at a very early stage of life.

———————

It is interesting to note certain common factors linked to the envisioning process in the case of each leader.

A leader's vision is always magnanimous yet simplified so that it can be understood by common men, who can participate in the formation and achievement of the same. Leaders take up challenges that call for the best in people and bring them together through a "shared sense of purpose". Most importantly, their vision is so large that it encompasses the smaller dreams of common people within. Leaders formulate a vision based on principles that become guideposts for humanity. They intuitively draw on the ageless wisdom and present it in a new synthesis to meet the particular needs of the times in which they live.

Envisioning trait is transformative in nature. It transcends from leader to those who follow him. A leader's vision involves large picture that is simplified enough to penetrate the ordinary mind. The vision travels through the time in search of achievement of ultimate purpose, bringing out the best the world has to offer.

A leader has the capacity to rise above the overpowering complexity of the world. He engages society with its competing, divergent viewpoints, and communicates effectively, sharing his thoughts and listening to others involved, so that their knowledge is built through collaboration.

A leader identifies and sets certain systems, processes, and principles to achieve the vision. Through his personal desire to make a long lasting contribution, he invests time, energy, and resources necessary to generate tangible results, thereby setting a personal example for others to follow. Envisioning requires total involvement, focussed, and disciplined approach, a willingness to put every imaginable available resource in optimal use and above all continuity.

A leader works with the power of desire and alignment with a higher purpose. He is a social innovator. Leaders successfully manifest their visions on an inspirational, positive picture of the future, and they have a clear sense of direction as to how to get there. Vision is a field that brings energy into form. They passionately communicate the vision to create a strong field which then brings their vision into reality.

Leaders inspire people to be better than they already are and help them identify their better part. Leaders transmit energy to people, giving them a new sense of hope and confidence in achieving the vision.

Their vision is a dream large enough, to accommodate many

small dreams. People believe in leaders because they see their own dreams being achieved through the fulfilment of a much larger dream.

*Can there be anything worse than losing sight?.........
........Yes, losing vision.*

—*Swami Vivekananda*

www.universalhunt.com

SELF-MOTIVATION/SELF-RESPECT

(Positive Attitude/High Capacity to Absorb Failure)

"A leader's conviction in vision and passion for purpose triggers highest level of self-motivation and self-respect, developing positive attitude towards every event in life. This enables him to stand tall as a mountain absorbing every failure, until he experiences success, that further strengthens his conviction, making him furiously self-motivated, naturally inspiring and influencing everything that comes his way in the pursuit of his goals. His self motivation makes him more humble while he swirls in the cyclone of success and failures with a smile on his face and calmness in his mind".

I tried to analyse different feelings one experiences at different times in life. It became clear that primarily, every feeling or emotion is related to either "fear" or "growth".

Life shrinks or expands in proportion to one's courage. Growth happens when we perform an action to achieve something that we do not have, something that is larger, in terms of quality, value, and concern and vice versa. When we merely feel the urge to grow, it pushes us to perform growth oriented actions that lead us to achieve something of a superior nature. Whether you generate the feeling of growth first and perform actions next or you act first and experience growth as a result, both situations would end up making you successful. The growth and the action are directly proportional to each other. The process is cyclic in nature as one triggers the other.

Feeling of growth is normally experienced when you are involved in an action which may be leading to your growth in terms of personality, knowledge, experience, production, skills, etc. Doing something constructive in direction of growth adds to the process of civilisation, and your own evolution as a person. Say for example, reading this book or spending quality time at office with colleagues and at home with friends and family, attending a seminar or anything that gives you a kick from within, make you feel delighted and elevated, correspond to growth.

When we perform actions to avoid loss of something which we already possess, it triggers the feeling of fear; and vice versa. When we are in a state of fear, we subconsciously move towards performing those actions, which are related to protecting what we possess.

One needs to consciously make efforts every time to remain in the "growth" mode removing any type of fear of losing anything. Once you are in growth mode you naturally leave no room for fear and all your activities are productive, constructive, and achievement-oriented.

"Impossible is a word found only in a fool's dictionary."
—Napoleon Bonaparte

According to me, this process of consciously keeping oneself in the state of growth is self-motivation. Let's understand how and why a leader remains self-motivated, and what all positive factor this motivation subsequently generates.

The more you lose yourself in something bigger than yourself, the more energy you will have.

Every leader is infused with a special energy, which he transmits to those around him. He has the capacity to energise every person coming in his contact. Leaders are so deeply motivated about their purpose, goals and actions that every move made by them is a reflection of that motivation. They have tremendous capacity to remain self-motivated under

The higher your energy level, the more efficient your body. The more efficient your body, the better you feel. The better you feel, the more you will use your talent to produce outstanding results.

all circumstances. It would be proper to say that a leader does not require any external motivation. Leaders possess a very high level of maturity and they condition themselves to face any eventuality or outcome. They neither become happy very fast nor get sad on loss for they keep a larger and bigger vision. On every achievement or success they immediately plan for bigger success instead of restricting their happiness to a certain level. When they fail to achieve something, they quickly engage themselves to adopt another method/s of achieving the desired results.

On achieving something, they never feel contented and do not get emotional. This should not be taken as they do not celebrate success but they quickly elevate the benchmark and move on in pursuit of the next goal. They take that as one more milestone unlike normal people who remain in illusion of considering that as final destination and ponder over it for long before they realise that there is more to everything.

One should not misunderstand this attribute of a leader to being greedy. They are actually not greedy but they have the capacity to think really big beyond their personal needs or requirements, lest they may actually stop thinking or aiming higher and get satisfied and slowly move towards regress due to lack of action. This would then lead to lack of achievements and feeling of loss. Something within them always drives them to achieve more, higher, better and bigger. They exhibit a splendid display of selfless behaviour as they carry the courage of moving beyond their personal domain and benefit.

Many a time the scale or capacity they talk of appears unrealistic but they end up proving their capacity to create the demand. They first plan the vision and then work backwards to create the demand. Their purpose compels them to remain highly active, and so much of action naturally puts them at higher probability of achievement. The feeling of success keeps them motivated, which in turn sets them to achieve the next milestone which is

Leader is a personification of that energy which generates, adds, multiplies, amplifies, and animates through self-motivation.

even more action packed, and so this cycle continues. The action packed life of a leader keeps him fully charged and hence self-motivated.

Leadership is a process of preparing oneself for multiple failures to achieve few successes. It is said that on an average an individual succeeds in one out of ten attempts and fails nine times.

Success is the leadership quality to go from failure to failure without losing your enthusiasm.

Leader is a person who is so deeply involved in achieving "that one success" that he almost overlooks and recovers from impact of other nine failures. Leaders are people who have capacity to absorb failures; success follows by default. If you have higher capacity to absorb failures you are bound to succeed more. People with low capacity to absorb failures normally stop attempting for success. If one develops capacity to fail 900 times, I am sure he would see 100 greater successes.

Success is situational and relative in nature. What is success for someone is failure for someone else, and what was success yesterday might be seen as failure tomorrow, and may again become success day after. Definition of success is different for every person, and even for one person, it is different from time to time and situation to situation. In order to achieve desired result, one needs to make continuous attempts in one or

Don't let what you cannot do interfere with what you can do.

more possible ways. The outputs which are not desired are failures. Instead of getting deterred by failures one must think that he has learnt one more way to avoid undesirable result in a particular situation. Sometimes an undesirable output under one situation becomes desirable under another situation.

Self-motivation is all about remaining charged in pursuit of what you want without settling for anything lesser than that greater achievement. Leader is indefatigable in nature. Success and failure are two sides of the same coin. Leaders appear to be successful people but in a way they are the ones who have very high capacity to absorb failures, learn from failures and bounce with multi-fold energy and momentum. These people keep planning their next possible actions, after every failure. They do not deter from failure and certainly not change or lower the aim.

If you fail to plan, you plan to fail.
Motivation has a lot to do with planning in disciplined fashion. Motivation and success go hand in hand. Self-motivation leads to success-oriented action and the resulting success triggers further motivation. If you cannot plan for success, you are already planning to fail. Success is all about more contingency planning. Leaders have very high level of resilience. Along with high emotional stability and strength to manage and absorb failures it is very important to equip oneself with enough resources (including financial) to absorb failures. One may be emotionally and mentally capable of attempting again and again but then one might get financially broke, consumed, and exhausted after several wrong attempts and is left without resources to try out different more correct options. Life is not about what happens to you but it is about how you respond to it. When Edison failed over 1,000 times to develop a bulb he said that he thereafter knew 1,000 ways through which he could avoid what he wanted. And he continued his attempts and finally achieved what he wanted. I am sure he must have planned resources to experiment thousands of time apart from being

physically fit or emotionally prepared while executing this task.

Choice of Purpose: Many a time people get de-motivated thinking that they have chosen a wrong career or they feel they would have been better off if they would have chosen another field or industry. They always repent on what they do not have rather than value what is available. Trust me there is nothing like right or wrong "choice of purpose" in life. I see successful people around me from every possible background, be it politics or religion or music or fashion or business or philanthropy or art or science. Take fortune 500 companies which are the most successful companies on this planet, you don't find all of them giving the same product or service. There is success in every field. One just has to decide what he wants and simply follow that with 100% conviction, which naturally comes when you are self-motivated. Every business can be successful and scalable, one should just have self-motivation to face failures and success automatically follows.

"Within each of us lies the power of our consent to health and sickness, to riches and poverty, to freedom and slavery. It is we who control these, and not anyone else."

—Richard Bach

A leader doesn't compare himself with anyone. He competes with his own self and gets most satisfied beating his own previous performances. A leader actually gets the pleasure out of the feeling of achievement, feeling of winning, as a result of which failures normally do not affect him because he is anyways evolved beyond the limit or resources that can affect him at an individual level. So no failure de-motivates him or puts him under pressure. He views the entire episode as an event for which he takes the responsibility. He is

> "Leadership is the other side of the coin of loneliness, and he who is a leader must always act alone. And while he acts alone, he also accepts everything alone."
>
> —Ferdinand E. Marcos

intelligent, smart, and emotionally stable to hold himself responsible for everything happening in his life so there is no question of de-motivation or blaming anyone else. He overcomes the feeling of winning fast and there is no room for feeling of loss. Once he is successful in achieving what he wanted, he elevates the goal, the performance benchmark for next success, and keeps trying until again he achieves that and undergoes feeling of success, with higher, bigger, and better output than previous success.

> "Leadership is the ability of a single individual through his or her actions to motivate others to higher levels of achievement."
>
> —Buck Rodgers

A person of intellect who has no energy to act fails in life. Leaders are the centre of energy. They are so much charged and passionate about their purpose that they always remain fully motivated and also ensure that whoever comes in close contact with them gets fully charged and motivated taking inspiration from the high energy and motivation level of the leader himself. I would give more importance to self-motivation than the ability to motivate, because however good a leader may try to motivate the team, if he himself is not fully motivated, he is bound to fail and end up de-motivating people who are following his vision. But, if a leader is fully self-motivated, there is hardly any requirement to attempt to motivate his colleagues. People automatically feel and experience that energy, hold confidence and comfort around the leader and join him in his purpose to achieve their personal goals.

Leaders never ask for a good work environment, but they create a desirable environment through their strong sense of purpose, clarity of thoughts, and by energising people around them by setting right example of themselves through their own actions and success stories over a period of time.

Leaders develop passions for ideas, ideals, or tasks that give them the enthusiasm to go for it even when others criticise, object, resist, or ignore an opportunity. Leaders are initiative and risk takers who have the capacity to transform their ideas or ideals into results that benefit others. They find opportunities in limitations too. They have the capacity to convert threats into opportunities and this process begins with self-motivation. All leaders rely upon their own instincts and establish an environment that motivates others; sometimes alone and in uncertain conditions. They must positively influence others to motivate them who in turn may become leaders over a period of time.

Very high self-motivation is a result of clear vision, passion and commitment for purpose, excessively positive attitude, high self respect, self-value, and self-assessment. Leaders cannot attract others unless they are self-motivated. Many individuals tend to

"Leaders must be tough enough to fight, tender enough to cry, human enough to make mistakes, humble enough to admit them, strong enough to absorb the pain, and resilient enough to bounce back and keep on moving."

—Jesse Jackson

have a propensity to be leaders, while some learn successful leadership behaviour and go on to be effective leaders. Leading is the ability to influence others in a group. Being a good leader takes understanding of what motivates others. Leaders want to influence things to continue or create change in direction of their vision. Either way it takes a person with self-motivation to do the task.

Motivation is nothing but the process of "need fulfilment". In order to be a leader, it is important to understand what motivates people around you. It is necessary to understand and identify the fundamental needs that subordinates, team mates, co-workers, and bosses have. All the people have needs, right from basic needs like minimum income to need for a deep social connection to friendship, etc. People want to fit in somewhere in the box of relationship (personal or professional) and feel the sense of belongingness. If a person around you doesn't connect with you through any proper relation (like that of a colleague, brother, sister, father, friend, mentor, guide, advisor, wife or brother), there is no channel of influence. Motivation is possible only if a channel of relation exists to influence a person. Best example of this is Gandhi, who was known as the father of nation. His capacity to connect with people was fatherly in nature. His message, vision, and principles were such whereby people could connect with him like one did to a father. His self-motivation was influential enough to positively motivate and empower the whole nation in the struggle for freedom from 300 year old British rule in India.

Another large category of human need is the need for growth and challenges. A worker lured to a job by high salary may find his job dissatisfying if he is unable to connect with other people at work. It is much easier to lead and motivate if you understand what people's undeniable needs are. Easiest way of all is simply remain self-motivated and committed towards your purpose which is large enough to take care of growth for all. All other needs against growth are small. If you take care of the larger need for growth other needs are automatically taken care of as its by-products. Until you achieve the right efficient process or activity which can result into higher productivity leading to faster growth, you need to remain self motivated and continue in the pursuit of achievement of purpose.

To remain self motivated and keep others motivated, you must keep greater vision, set goals for yourself, and build an efficient team to achieve the vision. There has to be something to pursue. Leading is all about making channels of energy transmission from leader to everyone who comes under his influence due to

"Most people never run far enough on their first wind to find out they've got a second. Give your dreams all you've got and you'll be amazed at the energy you exude."

—William James

capacity to self motivate and motivate others for achievement of inclusive vision. It means channelising self-motivation into practical use, i.e. to motivate others for doing something productive for collective good. There are many factors essential in keeping yourself as well as others motivated. A common factor is goal and nature of work synchronised in best possible manner. You might think that if an individual carries out a simple task he would become more efficient then it is wrong, it might be boring; rather a task of variety and full of challenges with possibility of feeling of winning at every stage would be more motivating, hence more efficient. Most people are grossly under-utilised due to lack of challenges, hence find their tasks monotonous, hence get bored and change the goal altogether with hope of variety. This is the reason why most people resign again and again, change jobs, people often even change businesses. What they require is challenge within the same goal.

One must learn to break monotony through challenges within the same goal and elevate the goals as and when achieved. That's how a leader keeps him and people around him motivated. His focus is not only on the outcome but also on the variety of attempts to get the outcome; as soon as it is achieved they elevate the goal looking for new methods to achieve the same. Having the ability to achieve goals can be very personally satisfying. Attempts by many within an organisation to achieve the same goal can also create stronger drive to be successful. As a leader, it is important to make sure that the goals are reasonable. If they do not appear reasonable from point of view of the weakest person in the group, break down the goal into smaller ones and achieve it in parts. The effect of having a goal that is impossible to attain has negative effects and it can cause discouragement rapidly.

When goals are eventually accomplished or milestones are reached, make sure rewards and benefits follow, it is important to keep people charged. Many a time a leader may have very large vision and long term goal (ten year plus), as a result of which he may not actually distribute the short-term gains available through the achievement of smaller goals. But this is not how everyone in the team thinks. Make sure that in order to keep the interest alive for all those involved, there is a reasonable reward system. Reward should not be excessively high because the party may not last long always and people involved should not get used to excessive rewards/incentives; else you are preparing a ground for losing them as soon as the situation changes. Goal achievement creates personal satisfaction and advantage in the form of knowledge enhancement, growth in emotional maturity, boost to self-esteem, etc. Additional rewards such as salary increases, bonuses, and celebrations are also good reminders that individuals are appreciated for what they are doing. Reward is also a double-edged sword because some rewarded activities will take effort away from non-reward areas. While focussing on parameters to set rewards it is important to quantify the non-quantifiable having long-term impact like quality and innovation else it is likely to get ignored at times. It is also important to keep observing and changing the parameters because parameters need to be changed with time in line with the final goal in mind.

Work atmosphere in general has a lot to do with team motivation. Following are some key points to be kept in mind in order to have a sound work culture:

- Treat people around you like your partners.

- Involve yourself very deeply in the selection process or designing selection criteria as a leader because that's where formation of culture starts.

- Take as many tests possible but avoid removing a person from team.

- Do not experiment with large sets of people especially in areas where you are not clear about outcome. Put people as interims in such areas, so that corrective measures can be taken, else it negatively affects the overall image of the organisation.

As human beings we copy. Once as a leader, you treat your subordinates like partners and care for them; by default this culture percolates down the line and prevails in the system.

Keep in mind that there is a difference in treating a person like a friend and like a partner. Latter is a more matured relationship with respect and responsibility towards each other and signifies a common goal which is most important. People observe and understand that they are being treated in a way that they perceive as fair. Any unfair treatment would result into de-motivation towards work and goal. Before you take any action think how you would prefer to be treated if you were in a similar situation and then act.

Everyone likes to have independence and worth when they work. Control is sometimes important, but then so is flexibility. There would be instances where you would be tempted to give immediate feedback on something going wrong. Avoid that temptation. Give a genuine feedback with the intention and purpose of collective growth. As a leader, you must learn to mentor and know when to say, what to say, how much to say, how to say, and most of the time even not to say.

As a leader, instead of worrying about motivating others much, just focus on growth, remain self motivated, and avoid de-motivating others; by default you shall find people highly charged and motivated for achievement of growth as you do. A leader is always fully charged to charge all those who come in his contact or under his influence.

Leaders like Henry Ford and Abraham Lincoln are the best examples to show how self-motivation can turn a normal person into a great leader.

Henry Ford (30 July 1863 – 7 April 1947) was the American founder of the Ford Motor Company whose Model T automobile revolutionised transportation and American industry. He became one of the richest and best-known people in the world. He was a prolific inventor with 161 U.S. patents under his name. Before Henry Ford, cars were not the primary mode of transport and were a status symbol for high classes. Henry Ford changed all by making the car accessible to everyone, even to the workers that built it!

Ford was not the first one to invent the automobile. The first automobile was designed in 1769 and it was powered by steam. At the time of Ford building car, there were about 250 other car manufacturers, but Ford had the dream to provide affordable car to every family in America. Many believed Ford's vision was unrealistic because early in the 20th century every car was made manually. This made automobiles expensive and affordable to a selected few. In spite of many competitors and cost-prohibiting expenses, Ford built his first plant in 1908, eventually making the automobile available to nearly everyone. Ford developed the moving assembly line which could build more cars per day. By 1914, Ford was building more cars per day than most competitors could build in an entire year. Between 1908 and 1928, he made more than seventeen million cars. Ford's Model T completely eradicated the concept of car being a luxury for wealthy and made it a necessity and accessible to all. When it was rolled out in 1908, it was affectionately called America's Everyman car. Henry Ford's intense commitment to lowering costs of cars gave momentum to many technical and business innovations, including a franchise system that put a dealership in every city in North America, and in major cities on six continents.

The key to Henry Ford's success was his self-motivation for creating an affordable automobile. His self-motivation pushed him to remain distinct from competitors, critics, and negative thinkers, enabling him to carve his own niche to

You can have anything you want if you want it desperately enough. You must want it with an inner exuberance that erupts through the skin and joins the energy that created the world.

build automobile using assembly lines, lowering the production cost to the extent of making the product financially affordable for the general public. Ford invented the dealer-franchise system to sell and service cars. This has now evolved as the way of doing business. Almost every large business has adopted this model to scale up the business and cut down risks and investments. Ford developed an army of dealers and service engineers to support Ford car user anywhere in America. It enhanced the reach, avoided major investments in terms of fixed capital and also created business opportunities for all partnering Ford as franchisee/dealer.

This all was the result of the self-motivated dream of one man. The manufacture of affordable cars for every citizen kick-started America's Industrial Revolution. Following are some important landmarks achieved by Ford through self-motivation:

• He invented the assembly line system of manufacturing.

• The world's first conveyor belt was developed in a Ford plant. It could manufacture a car in ninety-three minutes.

• There were more than 100,000 workers in the Ford plant itself. Manufacturing of cars at this rate naturally pushed up usage of fuel resulting into construction of gas stations everywhere.

• It also created a sudden demand for infrastructure in the form of roads leading to the creation of one of the world's best inter-state highway system.

• He brought in many revolutionising changes in systems and processes to support mass production and services. He was a strong proponent of exports and his cars were selling in thirty-three countries during a time when most manufacturers were more than happy with the domestic market.

• He managed to raise and rear the American middle class. By the late 1920's Ford owned rubber plantations in South America, a fleet of ships, a railroad, coal & iron-ore mines, and thousands of acres of timberland.

• Since 1925, Ford was also involved in building airplanes – the most well known being the Ford 4AT Trimotor – during World War I.

• In 1941, Henry Ford also showed the world how to produce aircrafts like the B-24 Liberator Bomber at the rate of one plane per hour. His labourers worked in twenty-four hour shifts.

In December 1999, Ford was among the eighteen widely admired people mentioned in Gallup's List of Widely Admired People of the 20th Century. In 1928, Ford was awarded the Franklin Institute's Elliott Cresson Medal. The United States Postal Service honoured Ford with a Prominent Americans series (1965–1978) 12¢ postage stamp.

Whether you think you can or whether you think you can't, you're right.

It is self-motivation which transforms dreams into realities empowering us to act while others hesitate, flounder and fail.

Regardless of one's background, education, and training, when a person is self-motivated obstacles are overcome, challenges are creatively faced and discouragement is derailed.

Abraham Lincoln (12 February 1809 – 15 April 1865) was the 16th President of the United States. He is most famously known for his successful endeavour of leading America through its greatest internal crisis in the form of American Civil War, preserving the Union and ending slavery.

To be yourself in a world that is constantly trying to make you something else is the greatest accomplishment.

By the time Lincoln was seventeen, he knew he wanted to be a lawyer. Born in Kentucky, he had less than a year of schooling. Every time he got a new job, he would focus on enhancing skills which would help him be a great lawyer in future. Wading through different professions such as of a shopkeeper, a postmaster, and a surveyor, he learnt the skills of honesty, fairness, accuracy, and precision in business dealings. He also learnt the art of getting along with a variety of people. He would borrow books from a neighbour in the evening, read them by the light of the fireplace, and give them back in the morning. In the year 1836 his dream to be a lawyer came to fruition. This shows that if your goal in life is clear and your determination is strong; even if you may not necessarily be doing the work directly in that context, you would pick best skills available out of any activity you may be doing. This would enable you to bring yourself close to your goal. When Lincoln was elected to the Illinois legislature by the Whig party, he skilfully debated in public and enamoured people with his art of oration.

On the path to becoming president of the United States of America, he faced many ups and downs. Sequence of events mentioned below is just a reflection of Lincoln's never giving-up attitude which was primarily a result of his self-motivation. In 1830, at age of twenty-two, he lost his job when his father moved the family. Emotional trauma and loneliness people experience on losing a job at times ends up changing their career goals in the search of a new job. In 1832 at the age of twenty-three, he was elected company captain of Illinois militia in the Black Hawk War. Because of his Black Hawk War involvement, he did not spend sufficient time campaigning and was defeated in running for the Illinois State Legislature. His business failed twice in 1831 and 1833 and he came under heavy debt which took him several years to pay off. He turned to politics and was defeated in his first try for the legislature in 1832. His sweetheart Ann Rutledge died in 1835 and he reportedly had a nervous breakdown in 1836. In 1838 at age of twenty-nine, he was nominated for Illinois House Speaker by Whig Caucus but did not win the election, because the Whigs could not garner enough votes. He then served as the Whig Floor Leader. In 1839 Lincoln was chosen presidential elector for the first Whig convention. He was also admitted to practise law in U.S. Circuit Court. In his early thirties, he was re-elected to Illinois State Legislature. Lincoln was also admitted to practise law in U.S. District Court. He emerged as a very successful lawyer, as well as a popular legislator. He lost in his first attempt to be nominated for congress in 1843. Despite so many defeats, he did not give up and was ultimately elected to congress in 1846. In 1848 at age thirty-nine, Lincoln's term in office was

> *My great concern is not whether you have failed, but whether you are content with your failure.*

up as he ceased to be a candidate for Congress, as per an arrangement among the Whigs. He did however try to get an appointment as Commissioner of the General Land Office at Washington D.C. but didn't get appointed. In 1854, he lost in the senatorial election. He was elected to the Illinois State Legislature but declined the seat to run for U.S. Senate. He was defeated in his efforts for the vice-presidency in 1856 and in 1858 he ran for the senate but was defeated.

Don't measure a man's success by how high he climbs but how high he bounces when he hits bottom.

Lincoln apparently had more failures than victories in life. But he understood that the real failure happens only if we stop trying. The only way to deal with failure is to learn from it and move on. When you slip, bounce back with full force.

The journey of life is full of unexpected pitfalls, disappointments and setbacks. Failure can either break us or make us. It traps the mind, preventing it to entertain possibilities of freedom and success. True failure happens only when one gives up.

Abraham Lincoln was able to free slaves in the U.S. states through the Emancipation Proclamation. He even tried to give voting rights to the African-American people. With efforts of such people today America has reached to a stage where the president (Barack Obama) is an African American.

One thing which is worth noticing in case of Lincoln is that he had a very versatile personality. He was very clear about what he wanted to be right from his very young age. He started making attempts in the direction of his vision at a very early age when most of people simply ponder and are afraid of making attempts fearing failures. Success is all about making continuous attempts even when one fails.

Having a clear goal and a spirit of self-motivation, gives tremendous courage to achieve the goal. The sooner you define your purpose of life, more are the chances of earlier and greater success.

> *Ability is what you're capable of doing. Motivation determines what you do. Attitude determines how well you do it.*

CONTINUITY

STABILITY/PERSUASION

A common thing you find amongst leaders is the continuity of determination, vision and motivation until they succeed. You can have anything you want, if you want it badly enough. You can be anything you want to be, do anything you set out to accomplish if you hold to that desire with singleness of purpose. One needs to continuously put efforts until one reaches an inflection point which gives sudden outburst of energy and speed in the direction of achievement of vision. That's by and large a stage when the vision that you had set becomes an all-inclusive vision and there is natural push from multiple directions in the direction of achievement of the same.

Continuity is the key to success and achievement. Most of the time we fail to achieve what we want not because we do not put efforts but because we fail to consistently maintain our focus and efforts in that direction. People have a habit of changing goals and not only that, the most dangerous thing is that unknowingly people keep changing their visions very frequently.

Due to lack of clarity and purpose in life we are not able to maintain continuity in whatever we do, especially in professional life, and the same stands true for our personal lives too. There is lack of self-motivation and confidence to stick to whatever we have decided and as a result of which we keep changing the purpose and the means. Ultimately we reach an age and stage after which it seems late and we retire discontented. Sometimes what we think as purpose of our life is actually not because in 99.99% of the cases, the purpose is set by someone else. We are bound not to grow if we need someone to set the purpose for us. Because we are subconsciously always in search of our own purpose we never remain committed to any purpose set by someone else. This leaves us unfocussed and this is why we end up giving up midway.

The secret of a leader lies in the tests he has faced over his entire course of life and the habit of action he develops in facing those tests.

This mainly happens due to lack of proper training, and mentoring. At young age there are several influencing factors which impress us and as a result of these impressions we make our role models in life and decide to copy our role models unknowingly. If you see a child, he perhaps wants to act like a batman or he-man or spider-man when he is young, then once he grows a little older his role models change, he no more jumps pretending to be spider man. Same philosophy or behaviour continues even when the person grows, only the role models keep changing. In early age, purpose of choice of role model has hardly any link with financial planning or desire for financial freedom. Once it is realised that the path chosen doesn't lead us to proper career planning, we change goals. Most of the time we choose a role model under the spell of glamour. People have the tendency to easily get impressed by an over-hyped act of goodness. I don't mean to say that one should not appreciate others but I would suggest that it would be fruitful to adopt best from all and create your own destiny rather than copying someone's circumstances, families, schools, colleges, social surrounding, locations, etc., blindly. You just cannot repeat exactly what has already happened. Even life and achievements of two twins end up being different! Most of us do not even analyse this before we leave this world. Some of us do realise, but it is usually really late by then. Even if we achieve our goals we do not enjoy the outcomes of achievements since we are either old or in no position to relish the success.

A leader, once convinced that a particular course of action is the right one, must be undaunted when the going gets tough. Once you are clear with the purpose it is easy to maintain continuity and keep scaling up the vision while achieving the outcomes and enjoying success. It is very important to give time to any goal we think of. If we see around us there are various types of successful people following various goals.

One can get overnight visible success after 10 years of continuous underlying and invisible work.

You come across doctors, politicians, religious leaders, businessmen, etc. Only common thing you find amongst them is not any specific choice of goal or career or profession but continuity of goals, determination and focus. If we keep changing our goals and do not give enough time to nurture and accomplish our dreams there would be no right goal. I personally would like to give more importance to continuity than the choice of goal. However, along with continuity, continuous improvement and elevation in attaining the goal (or scaling up) is required for success. Analyse your strengths, form a time-based logical vision, plan every possible type of resource for achievement and have unshakable conviction in it.

There is absolutely no shortcut to success. One needs to continuously put efforts until one reaches an inflection point which gives sudden outburst of energy and speed in the direction of achievement of vision. That's by and large a stage when the vision that you had set becomes an inclusive vision and there is natural push from multiple directions in the direction of achievement of the same. Until others who are a part of your vision genuinely do not develop that conviction, you keep away from that inflection point. Overcoming problems and repeated successful implementation of plans to achieve goals towards vision increases the conviction on means as well as end.

Many a time we may be correct in choosing our vision and goals in life based on our analysis of strengths and circumstances but we fail to devote ample time that is required for accomplishment of goals and quickly get frustrated. We need to learn to kill monotony in actions without changing our goals. Sometimes we get too tempted to do so many things simultaneously without giving enough attention or time to anything. We may end up taking wrong decisions.

A real leader faces the music, even when he doesn't like the tune.

"You only have to do a very few things right in your life so long as you don't do too many things wrong."

—*Warren Buffett*

Most of the time people simply give-up something and start doing next thing just to realise what they were doing was better. They lose one opportunity and start searching for something else and life goes on. This is applicable while choosing job, life partner, etc. So, do not give up anything that you are doing without testing waters.

We never get success when we chase many goals. Pursue one goal at a time, relentlessly; try different permutation combinations to attain success without giving up the end, experience cyclic changes in the surroundings while you are in one field, master the thumb rules in the same field and learn to scale up, get an idea of changes happening in that field/product/service, just get into it deep and make sure you get submerged in it completely. Stick to what you have planned and you are bound to get success. Continuity of efforts in single direction with different methods enhances productivity and helps you achieve desired output and move you in direction of success.

One of the most common causes of failure is the habit of quitting when one faces temporary defeat. Every person is guilty of this mistake at one time or another in his life. Continuity is nothing but building capacity against failures, success is a mere by-product.

Charles Darwin failed initially in his medical career. He was told by his father, "You care for nothing but shooting, dogs, and rat catching". Darwin wrote in his autobiography, "I was considered by all my masters and my father, a very ordinary boy, rather below the common standard of intellect". However, stability in following a purpose helped him evolve as an English naturalist who established that all species of life have descended over time from common ancestors, and proposed the scientific theory that this branching pattern of evolution resulted from a process called natural selection.

Winston Churchill failed in sixth grade. He was subsequently defeated in several elections for public office until he became prime minister at the age of sixty-two. He later wrote, "Never give in, never give in, never, never, never, never — in nothing, great or small, large or petty — never give in except to convictions of honour and good sense. Never, never, never, never give up." Winston Churchill became prime minister of UK in 1940 and received Nobel Peace Prize.

Albert Einstein did not speak until he was four-years-old and could not read until he was seven. His parents thought he was "sub-normal", and one of his teachers described him as "mentally slow, unsociable, and adrift forever in foolish dreams". He was expelled from school and was refused admittance to the Zurich Polytechnic School. He eventually learnt to speak, read and even do a little math. He ultimately evolved as theoretical physicist, philosopher, and author now widely regarded as one of the most influential and best known scientists and intellectuals of all time. He is regarded as the father of modern physics.

Henry Ford failed and went broke five times before he succeeded.

Walt Disney was fired by a newspaper editor because "he lacked imagination and had no good ideas". He went bankrupt several times before he built Disneyland.

Beethoven handled the violin awkwardly and preferred playing his own compositions instead of improving his technique. His teacher called him "hopeless as a composer". Most shocking to know is that he wrote five of his greatest symphonies despite being completely deaf.

Fred Astaire was an American dancer, choreographer, singer and actor. His stage and subsequent film career spanned seventy-six years, during which he made thirty-one musical films. After Fred Astaire's first screen test, the memo from the testing director of MGM read, "Can't act. Can't sing. Slightly bald. Can dance a little". He kept that memo over the fire place in his Beverly Hills home. According to Astaire when you're experimenting, you have to try so many things before you choose what you want and you may spend days getting nothing but exhaustion. There is the reward for perseverance. The higher up you go, the more mistakes you are allowed. Right at the top, if you make enough of them, it's considered to be your style.

When Pablo Casals reached ninety-five, he was asked by a young reporter "You are ninety five and the greatest cellist that ever lived. Why do you still practise six hours a day?" Mr. Casals answered, "Because I think I'm making progress."

Each person mentioned in the above examples is an unmatchable leader in his own field. They "never gave up" and that's the common point between all of them. They continued in their pursuit to make multiple attempts until they achieved success.

These are extreme cases of persuasion, self-confidence, and self-motivation which led to formation of leaders in their respective fields. Even basic continuity and persuasiveness can give phenomenal results.

Do not misunderstand continuity to be monotony. It does not mean doing the same thing again and again despite no desired results. It means doing different thing but without changing the ultimate purpose. Trying multiple ways of achieving what you want and not making the mistake of changing what you want.

Einstein defined insanity as "doing same thing again and again with expectation of different results". We are talking about doing multiple attempts until you achieve one pre-decided result, SUCCESS.

I would like to further stress on this by example of Thomas Alva Edison, who influenced the way we live and we would continue to live for years to come. His inventions touched almost every human being, not once or twice but almost every second. There are two major things to learn from him. One is continuity in pursuit of passion and second is size of vision, magnanimous enough to touch every life and bring changes in everyone's lifestyle. The products/services invented by him from an integral part of our life. Imagine home without electricity or light bulb!

Thomas Alva Edison (11 February 1847 – 18 October 1931) was an American inventor, scientist, and businessman who did many inventions and developed many products that greatly influenced life of all people of this world. His inventions such as the phonograph, the motion picture camera, and a long-lasting, practical electric light bulb, have changed almost the way we lived.

It took him almost two years of 1000 plus failed attempts, in his experiments of the different carbonised plant fibres, required for a carbon filament for his light bulb. During one of his experiments, Edison's laboratory got destroyed in an explosion. He got a loan from Henry Ford to build a new laboratory. Edison succeeded where others had failed. Edison chose to look at the big picture and created a lighting system including wiring, plugs, and connectors, to operate more than one light bulb at once. He was one of the first inventors to apply the principles of mass production and large teamwork to the process of invention. He is, therefore, often credited with the creation of the first industrial research laboratory.

Edison is considered one of the most prolific inventors in history, for holding 1,093 U.S. patents in his name. He also has many patents in United Kingdom, France, and Germany. He is credited with numerous inventions that contributed to mass communication and telecommunications in particular. His advanced work in these fields was an outgrowth of his initial career as a telegraph operator. Edison originated the concept and implementation of electric-power generation and distribution to homes, businesses, and factories – a crucial development in the modern industrialised world. His first power station was made at Manhattan Island, New York.

As he discovered his talents as a businessman, it began Edison's long streak of entrepreneurial ventures. It eventually led him to establish multiple companies, including General Electric, which at present is one of the largest publicly traded companies in the world.

Every vision, goal, task, action would have hurdles but what is important is to learn from every failure and go on with conviction without giving up.

Best part about a leader is his capacity to stir the thoughts of other people through encouraging words. I would like to share a few quotes of Edison that explained his philosophy of life. His quotes will leave you infused with strength, stimulate powerful thinking and change the way you look at life.

Many of life's failures are people who did not realise how close they were to success when they gave up.

The first requisite for success is the ability to apply your physical and mental energies to one problem incessantly without growing weary.

I am not discouraged, because every wrong attempt discarded is another step forward.

I never did anything worth doing by accident, nor did any of my inventions come by accident; they came by work.

Our greatest weakness lies in giving up. The most certain way to succeed is always to try just one more time.

Results! Why man, I have gotten a lot of results. I know of several thousand things that won't work.

Nearly every man who develops an idea works at it up to the point where it looks impossible, and then gets discouraged. That's not the place to become discouraged.

The three great essentials to achieve anything worthwhile are, first, hard work; second, stick-to-itiveness; third, common sense.

COMMITMENT

(Focus/Determination/Perseverance)

"Until one is committed, there is hesitancy, the chance to draw back, always ineffectiveness. Concerning all acts of initiative and creation there is one elementary truth, the ignorance of which kills countless ideas and splendid plans. The moment one definitely commits oneself, then providence moves too. All sorts of things occur to help one that would otherwise never have occurred. A whole stream of events issues from the decision, raising in one's favour, all manner of unforeseen incidents and meetings and material assistance, which no man could have dreamed would have come his way."

—W.N. Murray, The Scottish Himalayan
Expedition

Being decisive, focussed, and committing ourselves to the fulfilment of a dream, greatly increases our chance of success. One can see a very high sense of commitment in every leader. This commitment is an offshoot of greater understanding, conviction and respect towards their core values and vision. The commitment is not for their personal benefit but for the sake of people who have believed in their vision. No person with self-centred attitude can remain committed for longer duration. It is actually the underlying drive to achieve larger goal for the benefit of all that keeps one committed. It is important to understand in detail the thought process going in the mind of a leader as he remains committed and takes special care to ensure commitment of people involved with him.

Commitment means expressing loyalty, duty or pledge to something or someone. Commitment means spending maximum time or energy required to accomplish the task at hand without giving up or deviating. A leader inspires commitment by example, doing whatever it takes to complete the next step towards the vision. By setting an excellent example, a leader simply shows that there is nothing like nine-to-five job, but there are opportunities to achieve something greater.

Commitment ignites action. To commit is to pledge you to a certain purpose or line of conduct. It also means practicing your beliefs consistently. It means having a sound set of beliefs and faithful alignment of those beliefs through your behaviour.

We need to understand this trait in a little different perspective. There are only two types of people – leaders and followers. Every individual possesses traits of leader as

Each moment in life is either about convincing someone or getting convinced.

well as follower under certain situations. Even a leader can sometime follow someone under certain influence. Leaders also have role models. As mentioned above, "Each moment in life is either about convincing someone or getting convinced". This is a very powerful thought. We need to understand why leaders are able to make others follow in most situations. It is primarily a result of their own commitment to their beliefs and thoughts that is visible through their actions.

As human beings we all have some desire towards which we all are attracted. This desire or need gets developed over a period of time and it keeps evolving and changing with time based on our understanding, knowledge, maturity and learning.

As Maslow, a renowned psychologist has stated, our needs change, grow and get enriched with time.

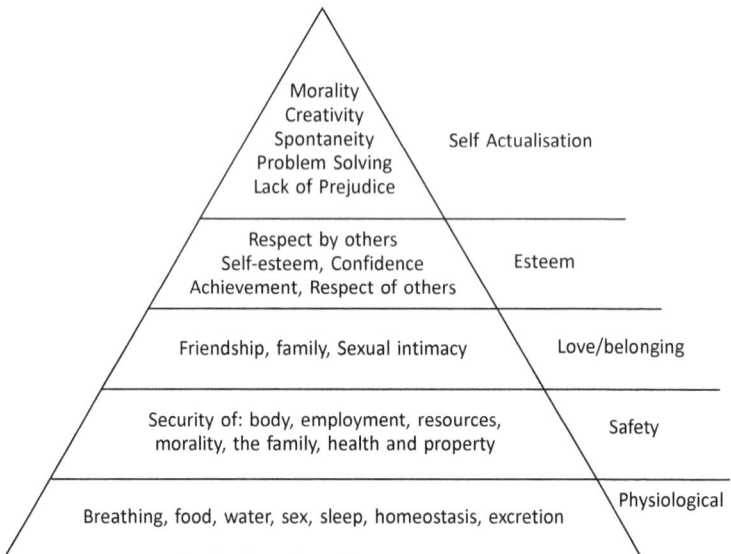

Our needs evolve from physiological to safety to belonging to esteem to self-actualisation. By and large, this order is observed but there could be deviations and overlaps.

It is important to understand the genesis, creation, and existence of needs. First of all, there is a desire which gets built to fulfil these needs. This desire drives our actions. Then there is "fear" which sets in. Fear of losing what we have gained and fear of being in a situation of not achieving what we wanted. In the course of our actions to fulfil our needs, we happen to interact with people and depend on them. We create a network of interdependent activities to gain what we desire. The more you want to achieve more would be your interdependence on others and more you would come in contact with people. You naturally end up coming in contact with people having similar needs and who are involved in similar activities to achieve those needs. When we are dealing with other human beings and getting dependent on them for our needs, we always fear if the other person would be non-committal towards the desired goal.

If a person is committed, he transmits highest level of comfort and trust in everyone around him. People dealing with him become dependent on him and rely on him once he is committed to a goal. Since committed persons are stable, they do not jump from one activity to another and hence it becomes easy for others involved in the task to rely on them, trust them and do not have any fear of losing them in middle of the task. That's how they naturally create followers around them.

Have faith in small things because it is in them that your strength lies.

Ensure that if you want to be successful, whatever activity you initiate, show full commitment and win trust of people around you. This way you shall emerge as an accepted leader. They would give you everything in turn. They would be equally committed and the task is bound to be completed.

When you are committed to any particular thing or task, you are bound to have more knowledge about it because unlike others who are not committed to it, you naturally spend more time learning things related to it. As a result of more knowledge about that task, others who desire to join that task naturally look upon you as a knowledgeable person and get bound to follow you.

This trait can be convincingly explained with example of professional life. People who are committed to their job naturally get higher responsibility because of the management skill and the amount of faith they build in those around them. As a result he also gains more knowledge about the company, product and culture. Rather, the person himself becomes the culture and reflects the culture. As and when more people join the organisation, people recognise that person as more knowledgeable, trust-worthy, and responsible and due to this they enthusiastically follow him. He ends up being accepted leader and not an imposed leader. He becomes a role model.

It is very important to understand that at very senior level promotions or appraisals or benefits are not based only on product knowledge or skills because at that level the competition is between people who are very experienced and proven in terms of technicality and subject knowledge. When a leader is to be chosen from among such competitive, successful and knowledgeable people then what matters the most is the commitment beyond personal interest towards the organisation.

As a result of unshakable commitment in their own beliefs and values, leaders naturally attract like-minded people to depend on them. They embody a sense of personal integrity, and radiate energy, vitality and possess a strong will-power. Will-power means standing in a spiritual state of being. Will is a spiritual attribute, which allows a leader to stand for a cause. More self-aware and reflective than others, leaders follow an inner sense of direction, and lead from the inside out, as exemplified by Mahatma Gandhi. Commitment develops trust and faith of people in a leader. It enhances their influencing capacity.

The impact of Mahatma Gandhi on the world has been extraordinary. He was an unprecedented example of a commitment to values, as he freed India by appealing to the moral conscience of Britain and using "*satyagraha*" (truth) or "ahimsa" (non-violence) as his actions. Due to his commitment of a larger vision in the overall interest of the nation and thought for freedom, masses followed him and were ready to even give-up their lives at his slight indication. His use of non-violent resistance in leading India to freedom inspired future leaders like Martin Luther King and Nelson Mandela, and set an example for freedom movements throughout the world. As a pioneer and strict follower of the philosophies of *satyagraha* and *ahimsa*, Gandhi's life is an example of unfaltering commitment to non-violence even in the most extreme situations.

As leaders we often underestimate the power of commitment, there is something powerful about being truly committed to a cause, to a vision or to a meaningful purpose. The decision to act on what you're committed to and passionate about starts a unique journey of discovery. You become more attuned to a new set of events occurring around you, you're more aware of opportunities, many of these events and situations you would have brushed off and considered as unimportant, your concentration on your actions is far higher than otherwise.

Have you ever noticed that when you purchase a new car, or a new watch of a particular brand, all of a sudden you begin to notice how many cars of the same brand are on the road or tend to notice people wearing similar watch as yours? It's not that they were not there before; it is just that you've become more aware and alert now! It all starts with commitment.

Success requires first expending ten units of attempts to produce one unit of results. Your momentum will then produce ten units of results with each unit of attempt.

Commitment gives ignition to momentum and it is about creating and sustaining momentum. It is a cyclical process of generating momentum and nurturing the same. Basis of commitment is to achieve something of substance. Through our commitment to our goal we seek to improve our financial situation, increase our emotional intelligence, and become physically fit. We work on our physical, psychological capacities and plan for resources.

Every goal begins with small steps. Overnight success comes only after years of hard work. Momentum is built through time and effort. You need to be persistent in your efforts even if they bring little improvement initially. If you are fully prepared while waiting for windfall gain or randomness to favour you, even a small event or slight change in situation may become an opportunity. You don't run up to a large rock and start pushing it with high speed. If you do that you may hurt yourself and it may not even move and certainly not in the desired direction. It starts with slow back and forth motion and then push in desired direction and once it rolls it picks momentum. Then efforts put are only to maintain direction.

People give up at times because events take their own sweet time, but leaders are persistent, they hang on. This is usually the worst time to give in as you are about to breakthrough to the next level and

One way to keep the momentum on is by elevating your goals to greater heights.

see the results. Breakthrough to the next level adds momentum and commitment for next stretch towards vision. And the cycle repeats until success is achieved until the momentum breaks through hurdles and obstacles on the way to success. Without commitment there is no momentum, and obstacles become stronger than your force.

One needs to have perseverance while working hard until you see some output. Often you may feel like giving-up but remember that you are creating momentum. Once you change your perspective it becomes easier and things begin to change. You would feel the change, however small it is, and that further enhances your perseverance and commitment. Success starts with commitment and perseverance, and over time you'll see the results.

As a leader, it is not only important to be committed but it is more important to ensure that everyone involved in the team shares equal level of commitment. It is very important for a leader to understand that if people cannot initially commit, it doesn't mean they don't care. They do care but are often caught up in a process of doubt. Understand difference between "ability" and "willingness". People are not "able" to commit but may be "willing". If leader remains indifferent to this situation people will neither be "able" nor "willing" to commit. It is that stage on ladder from where a person can neither move up nor is willing to go down and jumping is anyways suicidal. They cannot see beyond walls of vacuum, state of lack of information and feel confused, at times also de-motivated, and often give-up. This is where a leader comes forward sharing a vision, making them visualise the picture beyond those walls of vacuum, hence motivate them and comfort them to move ahead.

This process precedes every meaningful commitment. Leader is a fast thinker so is able to decide and express fast unlike others who take more time. Effective leaders catalyse this process, so that the critical mass of people can efficiently pass through this stage and commit genuinely with full conviction, knowledge and information, overcoming doubt and fear.

When leaders do not understand the commitment process they tend to seek accountability from team without providing information, and this is where people feel forced to commit. If this is not understood properly and people are pushed or pressurised, we end up with a team which is superficially committed. Later we simply end up losing people. Best way out in this situation is "Information and Transparency". Scientifically appraise the team with information required to fill in vacuum of unknown and be transparent in the process. Openly discuss pros, cons, benefits and possible failures. Update them on higher probability of success and hence logically convince them that it is all about taking "calculated risk" and not about taking a "chance". A leader is capable of establishing an atmosphere of trust and then within that atmosphere develops feeling of inclusion. Remind them of common vision we all had seen together, to achieve, grow and succeed.

Stay committed to your decisions, but stay flexible in your approach.

Leaders normally succeed or achieve their goals and fulfil

dreams or vision because they don't give-up. Having decided to do something, they simply stick to that. In other words, capacity to commit is nothing but capacity to absorb failures.

Capacity to commit is capacity to absorb failures.

Leaders do not simply succeed but they absorb failures and move up on the success ladder. Probability of success or failure is almost the same in everyone's life for every action taken over a longer duration. By and large, universe gives us all equal opportunities, what is different is the time taken by us to gather knowledge to come to terms with facts and look beyond illusion of safety. In a short duration of time, there might be more failures or more success but if we extrapolate the period to a longer duration, ideally more than five years by and large we all come across similar number of opportunities for success as well as failures. But only those succeed who have capacity to absorb failure. It is normally seen that if you attempt something repeatedly, out of sheer practise you achieve success. For every ten attempts, there is one success and nine failures. That means if you have capacity to absorb nine failures you will succeed once and if you have capacity to absorb ninety failures you will by default succeed ten times. Higher is your capacity to absorb failures, by default you enhance chances of success.

People who are committed have very high capacity to absorb failures, hence succeed naturally. They do not feel defeated and never think about failures, they simply keep moving in the direction of what they have aimed with much larger picture in mind. The clarity of vision and passion for purpose keeps them convicted and committed to continue absorbing failures and celebrating success, enjoying the whole journey that leads to fulfilment of vision.

I have attempted to explain this trait through two highly respectable and beloved people in their respective fields. One is a religious leader and other is the king of music. Their philosophy of life and profession is no different. Their work is their life. These are people who never had to fight with philosophy of "work-life balance". Their sheer level of commitment towards their profession reflects their life. They are committed to the vision for lifetime. If you observe, most leaders always have a very clear vision towards which they are deeply committed and this is the vision of their life.

Mother Teresa:

She was committed for whole life in service to humanity and global peace. Achievement of her vision in smallest possible manner was her satisfaction.

"It is not how much we do, but how much love we put in the doing. It is not how much we give, but how much love we put in the giving."

In 1979, Mother Teresa was awarded the Nobel Peace Prize "for work undertaken to overcome poverty and distress, which is a threat to peace."

Born in 1910, in Üsküb, Ottoman Empire, she was the youngest of the children in family. She was raised by her mother as a Roman Catholic after her father's death when she was eight. At the age of eighteen, she left home to join the Sisters of Loreto as a missionary. She arrived in India in 1929 and was disturbed by the poverty in Kolkata. The Bengal famine of 1943 brought misery and death to the city; and the outbreak of communal violence between Hindus and Muslims in August 1946 had created a ghastly atmosphere in the city. This is when in 1946; she decided to help the poor while living among them.

She plunged into the task of helping the poor in 1948 after adopting Indian citizenship. She ventured out into the slums and she started a school. She involved herself completely in the service of destitute and starving. Her first year was fraught with difficulties. She had no income and had to resort to hardship for basic things like food and supplies. Teresa experienced doubt, loneliness and the temptation to return to the comfort of convent life during these early months; but remained committed to her cause.

Teresa started "Missionaries of Charity" in 1950 with mission to care for "the hungry, the naked, the homeless, the crippled, the blind, the lepers, all those people who feel unwanted, unloved, uncared for throughout society". It began with thirteen members in Kolkata, and grew to more than 4,000 members running orphanages, AIDS hospices and charity centres worldwide. Caring centres for refugees, physically disabled, aged, alcoholics, and poor people were established. Victims of floods, epidemics, and famine were also cared for by Teresa. In 1952, Mother Teresa opened the first Home for the Dying where those brought received medical attention and were afforded the opportunity to die with dignity, according to the rituals of their faith; Muslims were read the *Quran*, Hindus received water from the Ganges, and Catholics received the Last Rites.

Under Teresa's guidance, several leprosy outreach clinics were established throughout Kolkata. They provided medication, bandages and food to ailing people. Mother Teresa started Nirmala Shishu Bhavan, the Children's Home of the Immaculate Heart, for orphans and homeless youth. By the 1960s she managed to open hospices, orphanages, and leper houses all over India.

Mother Teresa then expanded the order throughout the world and established another house in Venezuela in 1965 along with five sisters. Other establishments happened in

Rome, Tanzania, and Austria in 1968; during the 1970s, the order opened houses and foundations in dozens of countries in Asia, Africa, Europe and the United States.

In 1982, when the Siege of Beirut was at its peak, Mother Teresa saved the life of thirty-seven children who were trapped in a front line hospital by negotiating for a temporary cease-fire between the Israeli army and Palestinian guerrillas. She travelled through the war zone along with a Red Cross worker to evacuate young patients from the devastated hospital. When Eastern Europe experienced increased openness in the late 1980s, she expanded her efforts to Communist countries that had previously rejected the Missionaries of Charity, embarking on dozens of projects. She was undeterred by criticism about her firm stand against abortion and divorce stating, "No matter who says what, you should accept it with a smile and do your own work." Mother Teresa travelled to assist and minister to the hungry in Ethiopia, radiation victims at Chernobyl, and earthquake victims in Armenia. In 1991, Mother Teresa returned for the first time to her homeland and opened a Missionaries of Charity Brothers home in Tirana, Albania.

Let us not be satisfied with just giving money. Money is not enough, money can be earned. People need your hearts to love them. So, spread your love wherever you go.

She administered the operation of 517 missions in more than 100 countries by 1996. Over the years, Mother Teresa's Missionaries of Charity grew from twelve to thousands serving many poor and destitute in 450 centres around the world.

Imagine the kind of work she was involved into and the kind of work we do. Don't you feel what we do is far easier than what she was doing. It is worth thinking that what must have impelled people to join her in her cause? How she convinced people without any resources? No attrition, no expectation or aspiration management from team members, no problems of increments, no salaries, no grievance management, HR policies! Isn't it worth a deep thought? If not anything, we at least have no right to complain or get de-motivated. Don't you feel it is far easier to convince people in the work we are involved into? Why can't we create a team of 4,000 committed people to join us in the vision that we have? Why can't we internationalise our businesses to over 100 countries? We can, but for that we need to have a strong "inclusive" vision, passion for purpose and unshakable commitment to our vision. There is no shortage of resources of any kind whether financial or human, what is lacking is capacity to envision beyond personal benefit, an inclusive vision and self-commitment. Think big, start with small steps, and remain committed.

Mother Teresa was awarded the Padma Shri by the Government of India in 1962. She received the Jawaharlal Nehru Award for International Understanding in 1972 and the Bharat Ratna – India's highest civilian award, in 1980. In 1962, Mother Teresa received the Philippines-based Ramon Magsaysay Award for International Understanding for work in South or East Asia. In 1971, Paul VI awarded her the first Pope John XXIII Peace Prize, commending her for her work with the poor, display of Christian charity and efforts for peace. She later received the Pacem in Terris Award (1976). She was appointed an Honorary Companion of the Order of Australia in 1982, "for service to the community of Australia and humanity at large". The United Kingdom and the United States each repeatedly granted awards, culminating in the Order of Merit in 1983, and honorary citizenship of the United States received in 1996. Mother Teresa's Albanian homeland granted her the Golden Honour of the Nation in 1994. Universities in both the West and in

India granted her honorary degrees. Other civilian awards include the Balzan Prize for promoting humanity, peace, and brotherhood amongst people, and the Albert Schweitzer International Prize (1975). In 1979, Mother Teresa was awarded the Nobel Peace Prize, "for work undertaken in the struggle to overcome poverty and distress, which also constitutes a threat to peace." She refused the conventional ceremonial banquet given to laureates, and asked that the 192,000 USD funds be given to the poor in India, stating that earthly rewards were important only if they helped the world's needy.

When Mother Teresa received the prize, she was asked, "What can we do to promote world peace?" She answered "Go home and love your family. Around the world, not only in the poor countries, but I found the poverty of the West so much more difficult to remove. When I pick up a person from the street, hungry, I give him a plate of rice, a piece of bread, I feel satisfied. I have removed that hunger. But a person that is shut out, that feels unwanted, unloved, terrified, the person that has been thrown out from society that poverty is so hurtable [sic] and so much, and I find that very difficult." She also singled out abortion as "the greatest destroyer of peace in the world".

Her death was mourned in both secular and religious communities. She was a unique individual who lived for higher purposes. Her life-long devotion to the care of the poor, the sick, and the disadvantaged was one of the highest examples of commitment to service to our humanity.

According to the former U.N. Secretary "She is the United Nations. She is peace in the world."

A R Rahman:

A R Rahman is one of the greatest personalities in the world
of entertainment. His excellent contribution in music is
reflective of his tremendous commitment to music, which he
considers the ultimate mission of his life. Rahman redefined
contemporary Indian music and made it popular all over the
world. His passion makes him eat, think, breathe, and live
music. His extreme dedication and commitment made him a
megastar in the Indian Film industry. Let's understand what
makes him remain so focussed and committed.

For Rahman, music is not just a profession but 'a spiritual
experience'. He managed to change the very face of music in
India and infused a completely fresh style and skill to the
art. He has played a major role in popularising Indian music
at a global level. His fan following as a result is across
nationalities. After establishing the universal appeal in his
music, he has become an international icon. He set high
standards of music in India, inspiring every director and
actor of repute to work with him. In one of his interviews,
when asked what music means to him, he said it was hard to
define for it meant bread and butter, peace, happiness, and
devotion. He claims that there occurs a moment of magic
when something good emerges as a result of his constant
work on a piece. He finds immense joy by the fact that
millions find immense joy listening to his music. His
foremost attempt is to first like it himself and then take it
towards perfection. For him, music is beyond description and
without boundaries. According to him, when he sits calm and
blank, and prays to god, he receives divine inspiration to
create something original and out of the box. This is why it
touches million other hearts as well. For Rahman, music is
not a formula, but a spiritual journey. To bring out the most
soulful music, what is required besides proper knowledge of
classical music is a deep knowledge about life and
philosophy. When questioned about dealing with constant

pressures of delivering something different, leading to a burnout, Rahman replied that burnout occurs when one is not happy with what he is doing. This would be because he's doing it out of family pressures or financial hassles, but not as his passion. For Rahman, music is his passion, to fulfil which he naturally acts to create new, melodious and captivating music. This is the reason why he never felt like taking a break from his work. His passion drives him to study more about music. He feels that God has created him for a specific mission and it would be sacrilegious if he didn't fulfil that mission. He lives his life solely for music. That's his only mission.

His maxim is that only total dedication and concentration to one's profession can help in producing good work. Rahman is certain that this dedication must increase with fame. He always says, "My music has a mission. It has to reach the bodies, the souls of the millions for whom I strive to create it, music that springs from deep within me." He sets himself in the category of those men who love to seek refuge within. Rahman's music is effortless, comes flowing from within him. This is the purest form of music.

Rahman's philosophy of commitment to work best explains this trait in a leader which ultimately leads to success and satisfaction.

He collected innumerable accolades for his work including the Mauritius National Award in 1995 and the Malaysian Award for contributions to music. He was nominated for the Laurence Olivier Award for his first West-End production. A four-time National Film Award winner and recipient of the Padma Shri from the Government of India, Rahman has also received six Tamil Nadu State Film Awards, fourteen Filmfare Awards, and eleven Filmfare Awards South for his music and scores. In 2006, he received an honorary award from Stanford University for contributions to global music.

In 2009, for his score of *Slumdog Millionaire*, Rahman won the Critics' Choice Award, the Golden Globe Award for Best Original Score, the BAFTA Award for Best Film Music, and two Academy Awards for Best Original Music Score, and Best Original Song at the 2009 Oscars. Middlesex University and Aligarh Muslim University have announced that they plan to bestow honorary doctorates on Rahman. He has also won two Grammy Awards, for Best Compilation Soundtrack Album, and Best Song Written for a Visual Media. Rahman was awarded the Padma Bhushan, India's third highest civilian honour, in 2010.

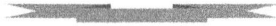

CHANGE MASTERS

INNOVATION/RE-ENGINEERING

"Men make history and not the other way around. In periods where there is no leadership, society stands still. Progress occurs when courageous, skilful leaders seize the opportunity to change things for the better."

—Harry S. Truman

Leaders define change. They can bring a change. They can manage a change. They can adapt to a change. They are not perplexed by the word change.

There are two type of events occurring in life, known and unknown. Most of us have a fear of unknown, which we define as risk. Nothing is constant in life. Everything keeps changing –

Different doors we open and close each day decide the lives we live.

people, systems, processes, society, and civilisation – and this process is evolution of mankind. We are all part of this change happening around us. These days with flow of information and advancement in technology things are changing much faster than people can even realise.

Either we should be responsible for a change or we need to adapt to a change. Leaders are trendsetters or change makers. They do not fear risk. They have an inherent ability to take risk as a result of which they take more number of actions than normal people. They work on different possible permutations and combinations. This behaviour results into certain mega events and outcomes which are responsible for major changes in environment, society, industry, and civilisation. They create new records. Rest of the masses, only later on realise the benefit of this and hence follow to grow equally so as to avoid being out of the race or perish. By the time they adapt, a leader again does something breathtakingly new and surprises the world. He is always not one but multiple steps ahead of others because he thinks ahead of time. A leader has the capacity to understand the larger picture and hence analyse the slow and gradual change happening in the environment around him. These people have the capacity to change before they are challenged by the change. They are normally trendsetters and they create change. They are responsible for change. In the event of unforeseen circumstances, if there is a sudden occurrence of an event, they can adapt very quickly depending on the need of that phase. They can mould themselves to that environment and if possible also challenge the change and set an overall new trend.

No one is a born leader or a perfect person, we all make mistakes but what is most important is to be self observant and take corrective actions.

A leader is not a person who never makes mistakes but they have tremendous ability to self observe, analyse and correct without any external pressure. They always look for constant improvement, elevating the benchmark.

Leaders challenge the status quo accepted by others.

In order to lead, it is important to be better than others whom you are leading. Some people develop certain competencies which keep them ahead of all. But with time, the so called competencies become normal traits as they are adopted by others and a person does not remain in strong leadership position. A true leader observes the change, analyses the demand or at times creates demand and keeps improving on his competencies and developing new competencies.

Genesis of being "change agent" lies in their capacity of self observation and self improvement. Leaders are knowingly alert and are attentive receptors of signals that are given to them in the form of feedback, reactions and reciprocating actions of people/groups/systems around them. They sensitively and consciously feel, analyse and act on these signals. They have corrective capacity to alter their actions if they find an action or decision taken by them is not in sync with the understanding or receptivity of people in the way they had expected.

Leaders know that change means growth. They have an inbuilt desire for growth, which pushes them to try multiple things to bring change in systems in which they operate. They make sure that changes keep happening for better outcomes, higher efficiency, better lifestyle, better business, and better results. Leaders ensure that change becomes an integral part of the systems and processes set. All those which adapt to these changes are followers.

Leaders are especially noted for transforming old mental maps or paradigms, and creating strategies that are "outside the box" of conventional thought. They embody a balance of right and left brain functions which are both rational and intuitive in nature. Their thinking is broad and systemic, seeing the big picture, the whole system, the bird's-eye view and the pattern that can be derived even in randomness. They then create innovative strategies for actualising their vision.

Leaders not only anticipate change but they create change. They are proactive to change rather than being reactive to events post implementation of change. Their focus is on opportunities, not on problems. They emphasise on win-win rather than adversarial win-lose approaches.

Leaders make people sway to tunes of music yet to be heard.

This trait can be best explained by ever innovating change agents. One is the Music Queen Madonna and other is king of technology trends, Apple's CEO Steve Jobs. I would rank them as one of the greatest change masters.

Madonna:

Throughout her career, Madonna has repeatedly and relentlessly reinvented herself through a series of visual and

Great leaders are rarely "realistic", in the beginning, by standards of other people.

musical personas. Her entry into the entertainment industry brought about a cultural change with fresh thoughts and trends that were never tried before. Madonna refashioned herself by working with emerging producers and unknown artists, while remaining at the centre of media limelight and climbed steps of success in entertainment industry. She introduced European electronic dance music into mainstream American pop culture. Her debut public appearance made her an overnight sensation. She has always kept herself abreast with the trends and has repeatedly reinvented her style with her preserving appeal. Madonna started a revolution amongst women in music. Her attitudes and opinions forced the public to sit up and take notice.

According to the International Federation of the Phonographic Industry, Madonna's 200 million albums have sold worldwide. She has been tagged as the best-selling female rock artist of the 20th century by the Recording Industry Association of America (RIAA). Madonna has generated over 1.2 billion USD in sales within the first decade of her career and thereby received acclaim as a role model for businesswomen in her industry. After its establishment, Maverick Records became a major commercial success from her efforts, which was unusual at that time for an artist-established label. After she made 26.6 million pounds in 2004 alone, Guinness World Records named Madonna as the world's highest-earning female singer.

London Business School academics called her a "dynamic entrepreneur" worth copying. They identified her vision of success, her understanding of the music industry, her ability to recognise her own performance limits, her willingness to work hard, and her ability to adapt as the key to her commercial success.

According to *Rolling Stone* magazine, "Madonna remains one of the greatest pop acts of all time". She has been dubbed as the "Queen of Pop", and is listed by Guinness World Records as the world's most successful female recording artist of all time. On 10 March 2008, Madonna was inducted into the Rock and Roll Hall of Fame in her first year of eligibility. She is the most successful female solo artist in British chart history, with the most number one albums and number one singles.

Steve Jobs:

A leader's innovation is not only seen in his actions but gets ingrained into the organisation and becomes very much an integral part of it. True success of the leader is only if he can institutionalise this trait into the organisation he is associated with. APPLE has been a great example of innovation at organisational level resulting in its emergence as an undisputed leader in the field of electronics. We are here not talking about improved products but about successfully commercialising "unused" products. What goes in building such companies?

> *"There are two ways of being creative. One can sing and dance. Or one can create an environment in which singers and dancers flourish."*
>
> —*Warren G. Bennis*

Three years after Chairman and CEO Steve Jobs had returned to Apple, the Company was having 3 billion USD market capitalisation. Its personal computer products had a loyal following in niche markets, but that was it. Over the past decade, Apple has launched five legitimately game-changing innovations iPod, iTunes, iPhone, AppExchange, and Apple Store. IPad is expected to be Apple's sixth big success by the time you would be reading this book.

Reflecting on Apple's decade of innovation highlights several lessons. Apple focussed on building beautiful products through new ways to create, deliver, and capture value. Competitors that chase Apple's latest release find themselves behind when Apple introduces its latest and greatest offerings after regular interval.

Steve Jobs has played a key role in Apple's success. Without such a dynamic and charismatic leader, Apple couldn't have become the most sought after brand that it is. Jobs gave Apple a strong mandate, pared down the product line, and tremendously helped the company focus on delivery. Apple's sole success has been through Jobs' relentless efforts. Steve Jobs' influence over Apple is undeniable.

Steve has transformed Apple as an Innovation Factory – one that harnesses creativity in its people, stimulates new ideas, and launches successful, groundbreaking products. Apple leverages its diverse culture, innovation processes, partners and networks to seize new opportunities in the marketplace and grow its business exponentially.

With numerous innovations, Apple has managed to increase revenues, profits and market capital multiple times in last decade. From 3 billion, Apple is now over 300 billion dollar company by market capitalization under the leadership of Steve Jobs.

OWNERSHIP

Grounded in ownership, guided by leadership, and informed by confidence and self-esteem; capacity development is the ability of people, institutions and societies to perform functions, solve problems, and achieve goals. Ownership embodies the fundamental starting point for improving people's lives.

Leadership in true sense means ownership. In simple words, ownership means "acting like an owner". He could be owner of the group, team, institution, company, party, situation or circumstances. I not only mean to say that people who are leaders act with ownership, which may sound obvious; but what I mean to emphasise is that every person who can take ownership can most certainly emerge as a leader. Ownership means growth. If you want to grow in life, take ownership of the situations. It is an indirect reflection of sense of responsibility.

Aham Brahmasmi or "I am Brahman" means "I am the Universe" which is the ultimate extension of ownership whereby you link and responsibly own every activity happening around you, in your life and beyond. By attaining a state of total responsibility towards each action, situation, circumstances and outcomes in your life and in this universe, you reach a stage of "zero complaining". You would never hold anyone responsible for anything happening in and around your life.

Let us understand this behaviour more carefully. There are by and large three types of activities we mostly engage ourselves into. Most activities are neutral in nature, routine, which would not make any measurable impact on the way we live, like routine work, food, sleep, etc., where systems are set, something which doesn't include major decision making or interdependence. These are mainly routine activities performed in past in "known" situations. These activities do not involve any risk. Here we are aware of outcomes which do not have any major impact on our life. These are the type 1 activities.

Type 2 activities include those which are not routine in nature and likely to give positive or favourable results. These activities are normally desirable and advisable to do; hence people make efforts towards them. These activities are known to lead us to growth, satisfaction, fulfilment, and achievement. Such activities involve decision making with outcomes towards positive side. These activities are well defined. Say in case of professional life, we all know that if we achieve extraordinary targets we'll achieve excellent incentives and promotions. Thereby we strive to put efforts in that direction. In case of personal life, we know that our better half would like if we present her with a diamond ring or quality time so we put efforts to see that million dollar smile on her face. If we are preparing for an exam or a board meet, we know the outcome of being fully prepared, so we put efforts in that direction. These are initiatives which we take consciously with anticipation of known outcome as seen in past.

Type 3 activities are those which are not routine, nor have any apparent immediate positive output at personal level and require decision making as well as risk. These appear risky because of lack of clarity of outcome. These are activities where it is never defined as to who will take decision for such activities. Activities falling outside Standard Operating Procedures or Key Result Areas or not linked to any advantage, gain or incentive. People who get attracted towards carrying out these tasks are called owners/ leaders in true sense. They normally do not ask themselves questions like "Is this my job?", "What will I get?" or "Why should I do?" These people instinctively assume complete ownership of the situation and execute the task. They do not display this behaviour merely because the task is not clearly defined for anyone and so they have to do. It is actually that at that moment decision making and execution is a prime need in the overall interest without any necessary personal benefit, which they clearly understand and perform.

Type 3 activities are "rare moments" or I would say "natural opportunities to lead". People with ownership attitude normally outstand other people, win trust of others involved, sometimes become role models, win respect, spread motivation and emerge out to be accepted leaders and not imposed leaders with titles. This activity could be as small as attending an unknown call from an angry customer. Leaders strive to give a proper response up to the satisfaction of the caller with an aim to improve the image of the organisation. The activity could be as big as attempting to save a neighbour when there is a fire breakout in the building, not being actually sure whether he would be able to make it or not, even in terms of his own life. It is such rare display of ownership without any expectation of return or result that carves leaders out of normal persons and they emerge as superstars. With time passing by, these people tend to take higher ownership elevating the scale of activity and become favourites amongst others. They become known, emerge as role models and start getting higher respect and natural authority.

Activity Type	1	2	3
Routine	✓	X	X
Known outcomes	✓	✓	X
Positive outputs	X	✓	X
Known timing (When to do is defined)	✓	✓	X
Involves risk	X	X	✓
Known to have personal benefit	✓	✓	X
Set systems and processes (How to do is defined)	✓	✓	X
What to do is defined	✓	✓	X
You are responsible for that (Falls under your "role" at "personal" or "professional" level.)	✓	✓	X
Frequency of occurrence	High	Low	Rare

Every leader starts with small acts of ownership and then owns responsibility of a large cause. He accomplishes the task with strong determination and inner drive from his core values.

It comes as a result of sense of responsibility. It is not assigned responsibility as a result of his designation or hierarchy but it is something which is responsibly assumed for the sake of betterment of the people involved and of those who will get involved directly or indirectly in future. It happens out of care for the people around. This sense of ownership gives feeling of achievement.

Normally people with leadership quality have amazing sense of ownership in any situation. They naturally feel tremendously responsible for completing a task undertaken. They don't wait for anybody's instruction or advice or direction to take charge of the situation, especially when there is a crisis at hand. It should not be supposed that they don't follow instructions or guidance given to them in a given task but they tend to perform "more" than what they are supposed to without feeling or making anyone feel that they are doing something extra. This kind of behaviour is normally observed or revealed in the time of difficulty or when situation is dicey. They don't wait for the instruction when an act is required in emergency and go an extra mile to execute the task, sometimes even risking their own lives.

Such behaviour is seen when an airhostess or a pilot takes charge of the situation in a plane which is hijacked, or forced to undergo emergency landing. This kind of situation may also be seen when an unhappy customer barges into the company premise and suddenly one of the executives tries to pacify him, listens to his queries and then tries to resolve his queries going beyond his role. Sometimes these decisions are taken by them even without any orders from their defined authorities. This they do in the best interest of the mission/ organisation so that the situation can be normalised as soon as possible.

Leaders always evolve. They are not defined or declared. In best of the defined situations, in best of the set key result areas and standard operating procedures; there is always room for them to emerge when something unexpected happens. There will always be a situation which is not predetermined or predicted. These are the times when "leaders" feel it is their duty to control the situation to avoid the worst and achieve the common goal of the group.

Such collective instances and various expressions of ownership differentiate these people from others. At these times, actions or outcomes are not important; what is more important is the "intention" and "intensity of involvement" of the person.

Such willingness to go an extra mile comes only when they have sense of care and belonging, which brings in them an intense feeling of owning that project or mission. They behave how an owner of the company or institution or project would have behaved. It is an immediate, impulsive, emotional yet logical move taken with best interest. It is not always necessary that the outcome of this move is as expected but the intention with which this move is taken is most positive. The leader strives beyond personal benefit with the expectation of positive outcome in the interest of larger purpose.

Normally while taking this action there is no expectation of growth or recognition. The action taken by the leaders is simply because they don't have tendency to wait for the instruction especially when there is no one to give instruction; or one can say that it is sensed that it might be too late before instruction is sought from the right person. Urgency of situation demands action. These are heroic moves which are driven by reflex actions and intuitions.

Such actions can only be taken by those who have the capacity to analyse the situation swiftly in a short span of time, who feel that they understand the situation and are relatively more confident of the positive outcome. Such people are intensely optimistic by nature. There is a feeling of helping others by in-time intervention when others are either confused or scared to take an action or simply feel it is not part of their job or none of their business.

In context of business, we can say that these actions are similar to those which an owner of a business would have taken. Ownership based actions are motivated by sense of ownership of the situation or problem. Leaders don't own this situation with any expectation of material return or expectation of long-term return but purely out of feeling of responsibility. It is not an action which is taken for self protection.

Leadership doesn't begin when you're given the position, power, or office. It begins when you take the ownership of the project, the people, and the problems. There are so many people in leadership "positions" but they aren't leading because they aren't taking ownership of the issues. They pass the buck. They don't take up the charge to lead the way. And as a result their business or their ministry remains stagnant.

People who have the power and yet sit on the fence are not really the leaders. They merely remain under the illusion of being leaders just because they have leaders' designation and are even paid for it. Their incapacity to be responsible towards the issues and their incompetence to motivate the team makes them unfit for their position. True leaders neither wait for others to show the vision nor do they wait for "designated leaders" to recognise the problem and give them permission to look for its solutions. They make efforts to make the problem visible to all and thereby create awareness. They escalate and resolve. If you're waiting for people to "get it", you are not a leader. Leadership begins with ownership. Embrace the issue that no one else sees. Call your people and your resources to bear on something that everyone else has neglected. Don't let it go until it is done. Hold people accountable. Live like it is a reflection on you, because it is.

Best way through which leaders execute ownership is by reaching where the problem is and by finding the solution for it. Learning happens maximum where there is a problem or a challenge. What others define as problem is nothing but an unknown situation whose outcome cannot be predicted. Given our human nature there is tendency to predict negative outcomes when outcomes are unknown but we must remember that probability of good and bad outcome is always 50% irrespective of the situation, whether known or unknown. The moment we address an issue, situation does not remain unknown and that's the process of evolution that we define as experience. By facing an unknown situation, we enhance our experience, maturity, and knowledge faster as compared to others who prefer to avoid unexplored domains simply out of fear of negative outcome. Reach first where there is challenge and face it. It is an owner's job to execute all those functions which do not fall into the preview of defined job role.

I would like to highlight this trait through two such splendid displays of ownership that are in contrast to each other. One is a heroic act of ownership with selfless intention, and second is a task though not heroic in nature but helps you identify a "hero in making". Always look for "heroes in making" in your team/organisation and lavishly recognise them, support them, authorise them and promote them.

Mumbai, the Financial Capital of India, was under terrorist attack on Wednesday, 26 November 2008. One of the spots under attack was Hotel Taj Mahal Palace and Tower. Karambir Singh Kang was appointed as General Manager of Taj Mahal Palace and Tower in November of 2007. On 26/11, as the fire and the gun battle raged inside this iconic hotel of Mumbai, the flaming façade concealed a story of incredible loss and heroism.

Trapped inside the burning sixth floor was the family of Karambir – his wife Niti and two sons – fourteen-year-old Uday and five-year-old Samar. Karambir watched helplessly as the fire devastated the floor; he had no access to them because of the ongoing encounter. By Thursday morning it was clear that only a miracle could save his family and others on that floor. The sixth floor burnt down to a cinder, and with no way to escape, Karambir's wife and two sons died of asphyxiation. He found the courage to stand his ground – to battle his own terrible tragedy, and help the evacuation process so that others may live. He stayed inside the Taj till Saturday afternoon, supervising the rescue operations and helping the armed forces in every possible way.

Even in the face of the greatest personal loss, Karambir never lost his courage, or his will to help save the lives of others who were stranded. Many people owe their lives to the efficiency of Karambir, who personally supervised operations to ensure that maximum lives could be saved.

No matter how elaborate is your planning, no matter how sophisticated are your systems, no matter how intensive is your training, ultimately all boils down to how committed you are and how much ownership do you take in anything that you do.

On 20 January 2009, the global hotel industry joined India in a ceremony where Karambir received the special award of Corporate Citizen of the Year. When Kang walked onto the stage, the room rose as one and clapped hard and long. Many of the CEOs had tears in their eyes and Prime Minister Manmohan Singh was also full of respect and honour for Karambir.

Characteristically, Kang's acceptance speech was free of sentimentalism and any mention of personal loss. He said he was honoured to accept the award on behalf of his "Taj family", a choice of phrase which had a rare poignance. "This recognition is not just an honour for the staff of the Taj, but recognition of the true spirit of India", he said. "For any employee of our hotel, no amount of training could have prepared us for what we went through during those fateful days. They were all ordinary people, be it at the Taj, Trident, CST or Cama Hospital, with extraordinary courage who went beyond the call of duty. On behalf of my entire Taj family, I humbly accept this honour. Thank you."

I don't think ownership could have been better explained than this example. During such incidents of heroism, ownership is easily identifiable but there are many smaller incidents happening around us where we need to sensitively observe to find such heroes/owners in the making.

I want to share with you an incident that happened in my company, where a commendable act of ownership was displayed by an executive who had joined as trainee a month before this incident.

Once there was an electricity failure in the office and all

came to know that the admin person had not paid the bill. It had lapsed due to bill being misplaced and hence the power got disconnected. In such situation, the amount was to be paid in cash and the head office was located at a different place and branch manager could not be contacted. All the transactions are always done by cheque with little amount available as cash. In such case when everyone was calling head office and trying to figure out how cash can be arranged from the head office, one of the trainees rushed to the nearest ATM, withdrew the amount required from his personal account, personally went to the collection centre of the power supplier and deposited the amount against the account number of the company. He sensed the urgency of the situation and managed the work which otherwise would have suffered in the absence of electricity until funds were arranged. This was a perfect example of act of ownership. He acted beyond defined purview of job role in the positive interest of the company with 100% authority and responsibility which only an owner could have assumed. Moreover this person was not even on the payroll of the company and was under probation period. Thereby his efforts are more commendable.

Most of the time in a group of people, even when there are defined leaders, there are very few decision makers or owners. Mostly people wait for the decision to come from higher authorities. Where systems and processes are set, there is no question of ownership or decision making but this need mainly arises in areas undefined. It is wrong to assume that decision in areas undefined would come from top. You may as well decide taking ownership and escalate the matter or discuss out with others. I am sure it would be appreciated and your value in the organization would enhance and more than that you would feel more confident. Ownership is mainly about decision making in undefined areas. Unless you own the situation, you would keep finding someone responsible to take decision. What stops you from assuming responsibility? Just go ahead and do it.

Ownership is a character that doesn't deter a leader even in worst situations like recession. They presume themselves as owners of situation; they hold themselves responsible for everything happening in and around them, positive as well as negative. Hence they do not consider themselves separate from the organisation or feel negative. Under this situation they act most mature and productive unlike others whose performance deteriorates under pressure or lack of clarity. This becomes cyclic and leaders not only survive the bad times but outshine in bad times.

People who think and act like owners are happier, healthier, and more effective in every task or decision they carry out. This can simply be developed by assuming responsibility for their own behaviour, mistakes, and results, rather than attributing it to circumstances, economy, or seniors in the company. Start making selfless decisions and communicate in a way that reflects your care for the organisation, as an owner might do, probably strike you as oddly out of sync with reality.

Most of the senior executives have a habit of behaving like passengers and not drivers. The underlying assumption is seen oriented towards "they", rather than the "we" mentality.

When the time is good and when there are clear guidelines, defined methods and planned targets/goals, everyone is productive and puts efforts in defined directions by defined methods; but when situation is unclear, it is only people with ownership who take the lead, assume command, do not fear, take decisions, risks and move ahead in the race. They never slow down.

If you want to identify leaders with ownership quality, you would normally find them in voluntary groups. Leader of a community or society or a religious institution or sports club where designations are not defined, people assume natural leadership. These are pure gestures of actual leadership and these leadership positions are assumed without any direct or presumed professional benefit. Such leaders normally evolve. These are people who are liked by others due to their high energy level and optimistic approach. They do not take ownership because they want to become owners but they naturally assume themselves responsible for a task/situation, etc. So others naturally follow them for selfless decision-making in the interest of the group. It is the most non-selfish display of responsibility.

It works, if you work it. Once you start "thinking like an owner", rather than worrying about what "they" think, and when "they'll" appreciate your contributions, opportunities for you would become apparent to you. As a person newly in the "driver's seat" becomes more creative, engaged, and happier will as a result start caring less about what others think or might say.

As a leader, keep one thing in mind, you are working only for yourself. The only person on whom you are doing a favour is yourself. Even if you are doing overtime, it is not for company, it is for your own self; similarly if you do something less productive, the loss is not to company but only to you. Company is made-up of people and not bricks and machines, so whatever you do, it will influence your own growth.

Very recently, a friend asked me as to what he should do as he did not get a hike during his annual appraisal. He asked if he should take additional responsibilities. My answer was very simple. I told him, "What would you have done if your business would have not made desired profit, would you have put additional efforts? If yes, then don't shy away from additional responsibility."

Taking additional responsibilities in an organisation has nothing to do with appraisals or salaries. We take additional responsibilities to get more experience, to become sharper, smarter, and sensible and make more use of infrastructure and platform available. Higher the responsibilities you take more you shall learn and more would be your probability of success and more close you would come to achieving your goals, including financial goals. You are likely to do more damage by reducing your responsibilities which may result into making you less smart, sharp and acceptable.

If we all think like owners for our respective companies, we can even save ourselves from recession ensuring sustainable growth. Keep one thing in mind that recession is nothing but mass change in perception of future and infusion of selfishness. It is hunt for security at mass level across verticals and industries and institutions. In order to safeguard individual interests, we stop expenditure and reduce consumption to bare minimum level resulting into major slowdown in the rate at which money changes hands. It is a vicious cycle and it continues until there is some kind of major information inflow at global level which starts changing the perception of people. Similar kind of situation happens even at organisation or company level in bad times.

We all very well need to understand that an organisation is made up of us and not one person versus the rest. In a company, the moment there is some bad news about performance or large order going to competitor, there is a spur of movement realised. People start jumping the boat even much before it even begins to sink and most of the time they find themselves in more stable appearing but less reliable boats!

Imagine yourself in a family business headed by your father. You are one of the sons supporting him in the venture. Now you come to know that the competitor in the same product has done ten times more business than your company. What would be your immediate reaction? Would you get into understanding the reason for success, identify success strategy, promise yourself to beat up the competition, multiply your efforts to do all you can to beat competition, make a multi prong strategy, talk to all vendors, talk to all buyers, do market scan, take best people ... or ... float your CV to the competitor company? And I am sure sending your CV to the competitor company would be like a moral public death, a suicide for you! Why people don't think the same way when it comes to a job? Why people get tempted to get into another organisation when their organisation does not do well. Why can't they take responsibility of their contribution in the organisation's bad performance? Why they do not do something to improve the existing condition rather than changing job. These all questions need to be given a deep thought by all involved in running the organization. Mind well if you can't succeed in one organisation by and large you won't succeed in the other too. You should not be hunting for the "right" environment but you should be capable of creating the right environment around you. You should not be hungry after a so called brand but should have the capacity to create a brand. One just needs to think it with a different perspective and adopt a totally different mindset.

Once everyone starts behaving like an owner, the team gets "continuity" and "collective strength", drastically enhancing the productivity. In good times every one by and large behaves like an owner and takes pride in belonging to the team. Can you associate yourself with the team or organization with same pride even in bad times? If yes, then you are the owner. It indicates your maturity to take responsibility and keep your commitment to overcome the worst. There is no big deal if you join a big brand or group but there is a BIG deal if you can create a big brand out of an ordinary brand. Leadership just can't begin without ownership. One can just not scale up, or maintain continuity in efforts, without owning the purpose and situation associated with that purpose.

Many corporate make several attempts and take several steps to infuse ownership at different levels but according to me ownership evolves, it can never be infused. Many a time when the designated leaders fail to display ownership, companies come out with special projects involving people from different expertise and hierarchies across division where all have equal say. It is relatively easy to bring out character of ownership under such model. However a real owner does not necessarily need any facilitation to express his ownership. He would consider himself the owner under every situation and will hold himself most responsible for things happening around him. He will consider importance of his influence in day-to-day happenings of the group.

Ownership is normally seen when there is a very clear sense of purpose. Until one finds clarity in the purpose by linking his presence with future outcomes of actions, and achievements of goals at larger level, ownership never comes out. Many at times we find designated people associated with an organisation without a fire of ownership because they do not sense achieving any major outcome using that platform or have lost the passion to achieve. But you may find a person new to the team sprawling with ownership since he may relate his being in that team with the purpose of using that platform to achieve the same.

The individual increasingly comes to know who he is through

the stand he takes when he expresses his ideas, values, beliefs, and convictions and through the declaration and ownership of his feelings.

> *Ownership is exercise of control and command, from the idea to the process, from input to output, from ability to results.*

PASSION

INSPIRATION/ENERGISING/DESIRE/INFLUENCING

To have long term success in any position of leadership, you have to be obsessed in some way with something. Leader is someone who is insanely obsessed with his larger vision making it his purpose of life. He pursues every small goal to fulfil larger vision and persistently involved in actions to achieve the set goals. He reviews and monitors actions and outcomes of actions in alignment with goals, reworking on deviations and setting fresh and higher goals in direction of larger vision. Many a time the vision also takes finer larger shape as goals are achieved.

www.universalhunt.com

As a result of the capacity to envision and define clear goals, a leader develops tremendous clarity of thought and capacity to develop process to implement actions and achieve goals, thereby fulfilling his vision.

Passion is nothing but "strong sense of purpose" which makes a leader determined about every action and desirous of its output. Very high sensitivity to the purpose triggers high level of motivation keeping him undeterred by failures. This entire cycle of actions in the pursuit of goals keeps him highly motivated, energised and involved.

Leader is someone who is insanely obsessed with his larger vision making it his purpose of life, perusing every small goal to fulfil larger vision and persistently involved in actions to achieve the set goals. He reviews and monitors

"If a man hasn't discovered something that he will die for, he isn't fit to live."

—Martin Luther King

actions and outcome of actions in alignment with goals, reworking on deviations, and setting new fresh higher goals in the direction of larger vision. Many a time the vision also takes finer larger shape as goals are achieved.

This process keeps him involved, making him the centre of actions. When all this is happening there are many people around him involved with their own actions and beliefs because of their desire to fulfil their smaller dreams. A leader needs to constantly keep simplifying his vision and goals for the benefit of the people involved, and ensure that the actions and tasks are being carried out as planned. In the process, the leader starts enjoying this gamut of actions, speed, involvement, people believing in him, success, failure, motivation etc.

He is so much involved in this process that the vision keeps taking a larger shape and people involved keep achieving their smaller dreams adding larger base of followers giving greater sense of fulfilment and achievement. This display of soundly oriented actions around a vision and deep involvement of oneself into this process till the vision is realised is called passion.

Leaders do each of their activity passionately because through these activities they try to achieve their goals and hence vision, which gives them sense of achievement, happiness, and defines their overall purpose of life.

Passion springs from a combination of belief, enthusiasm, and emotion. When someone is passionate about something, he is

Passion is transfer of emotions which wins the hearts and minds of listeners.

filled with excitement and zeal, and wants to share it with the world. He can't be deterred by the opinions of others and is excited to convert as many people to his cause as possible. There is a sense of mission that drives him, that stimulates his imagination, and that motivates him to higher levels of achievement. Passion alone can be effective in influencing opinion and in getting people to support product, service, or cause. More than anything else, passion wins the hearts and minds of listeners. When people sense passion and heartfelt conviction for cause or product, they emotionally jump on board. We all love people who are excited, animated, and full of passion. Passion is a transfer of emotion.

Nothing great was ever achieved without passion. Passion is the great moving force of spirit and energy that permeates all we do. It is the force that keeps motivation going until a goal is reached. When one gets passionate, the entire personality lights up, the mind becomes sharper, more intuitive; entire life force and creative ability are enhanced. Such a person is motivated and certainly makes an impact.

Leadership is passion. Without passion, a person will have very little influence as a leader. I believe passion provides an individual with the light of leadership and creates an undeniable drive to make a difference. Consider the legacy of historical leaders like John F Kennedy, Mother Teresa, and Abraham Lincoln. They are regarded as great leaders because they worked with passion for the purpose.

Passion is essential to the happiness of an individual, whether they are working for a large corporation, volunteering for a non-profit organisation, or developing their own business. After all, humans naturally desire to make a positive contribution to society; a lasting impact on both the present and future. I believe great leaders recognise a need, draw upon it, and use it to engage individuals in their cause. Essentially, they draw others to the flame of their passion and in turn ignite passion in others.

In all great leaders there is a purpose and unmistakable intensity. A man who merely wants to be liked will never be a leader. A broad examination of history shows clearly that men follow those they respect. Respect is recognition of inspiration, purpose, competence and personal force or power. Passion is a self-generated tool. You have the ability to motivate yourself; to concentrate on your purpose; to get yourself excited about what you do. Your attitude sets the mood for everyone around you. They get excited if you are excited. If you are fascinated, so are they. Recommendations

"Absolute identity with one's cause is the first and great condition of successful leadership."

—Woodrow Wilson

you give to others that come from the heart have a greater impact. Everyone can increase their purpose and intensity. When you organise all of your activities toward one focussed goal, you not only feel more joy in what you are doing, you get more accomplishment. Sometimes it helps to find things that make you passionate. There is nothing stronger than a leader with a firm direction and passion to reach his goal.

The key to successful leadership is influence, not authority.

Passion generates power to inspire, influence, and impress anyone and everyone who comes in direct or indirect contact. People want to be inspired. In fact, there is a whole class of people who will follow a passionate inspiring leader. Inspiring is usually just a matter of communicating clearly and with passion, impacting others' thoughts, actions and life as a whole. Inspiring means showing others the picture that you want them to see, a larger picture that transcends your passion into them. Inspiring is a process of transfer of energy from one person to another. A leader is so much charged with energy that he has the capacity to infuse others with the same energy and set them in the desired action ultimately leading to a much larger goal. They help others in expanding their horizons, show them a larger picture, and take them through a passionate journey of desire and success.

A great example of inspiration is when Steve Jobs brought the CEO from Pepsi to his own company by asking him, "Do

Leadership is getting someone to do what they don't want to do, to achieve what they want to achieve.

you want to sell sugar water for the rest of your life, or do you want to change the world?" The founder of Jefferson Standard built a successful insurance company from scratch. He assembled some of the greatest insurance people by simply asking, "Why don't you come and help me build something great?"

Leaders are good at inspiring people through stories and examples. Stories can be examples from your customers, "fictitious" examples from your life, or even historical fables and myths. Stories help you vividly illustrate what you are trying to communicate. Stories that communicate on an emotional level help communicate deeper than words and leave an imprint much stronger than anything you can achieve through a simple stating of the facts. This essentially works because of a leader's capacity to understand the need of an individual.

A leader not only has the capacity to see the larger picture but he also sees through people at mass as well as individual level. He is able to sense their needs and connect their today's needs to the larger picture at the same time elevating their current needs through infusion of desire in them, by making them capable of dreaming bigger. They are good at simplifying complex looking things and making the larger picture look simple which used to appear tough or non achievable.

Let me simplify the understanding of this trait by example of a person who I feel was most passionate about his purpose, profession, disposition, speech and life as a whole. He was most influential and inspired everyone who saw him or heard him. Anything he did couldn't go unnoticed and literally pulled people in the flow of his passion! He is certainly one of my role models for intensity of passion.

Michael Jackson:

Michael Jackson (29 August 1958 – 25 June 2009) was an American singer-songwriter, dancer, actor, choreographer, poet, businessman, philanthropist, and record producer. Referred to as the "King of Pop", he is recognised as the most successful and influential entertainer of all times. His unrivalled contribution to music, dance, and fashion, and a much-publicised personal life made him a global figure in popular culture for over four decades.

Jackson made his debut in 1964 as the lead singer of The Jackson 5. He started his solo career in 1971, and created ten studio albums. Of these, the 1982 album Thriller became the best-selling album of all times, having sold more than 110 million copies worldwide. Four of his other albums Off the Wall, Bad, Dangerous and History: Past, Present and Future, Book I (best-selling double-album of all time by a solo artist) ranked among the world's best-sellers making Jackson a world famous celebrity. His 1997 release, Blood on the Dance Floor: History in the Mix, is the best selling remix album of all times.

His distinctive musical style and choreography transcended generational, racial and cultural boundaries. Jackson is known for elevating the music video from a mere promotional tool into an art form. He created groundbreaking videos for songs such as Billie Jean, Beat It and Thriller – the last of which has been voted as the greatest music video of all times. The video for "Thriller" is the only music video inducted into the national film registry in the Library of Congress where inductions are preserved forever. He was the first African American artist to gather a strong crossover following on MTV. Jackson's music videos facilitated the promotion of MTV and Cable TV. Jackson popularised a number of complicated dance techniques, such as the robot and the moonwalk.

Jackson has been inducted twelve times into various music halls of fame and is one of the very few artists to have been inducted into the Rock and Roll Hall of Fame twice. Other achievements include thirteen Guinness World Records, more than any other artist, and including the Most Successful Entertainer of All Time; fifteen Grammy Awards, including the Living Legend Award and the Lifetime Achievement Award; twenty six American Music Awards more than any other artist, and including recognition as Artist of the Century; seventeen number-one singles in the United States and over 780 million record sales globally.

Michael Jackson radiated Power of Passion. He was icon of influence with capacity to influence people with his music. His ever oozing passion was like red hot volcanic lava which never cooled off even after his death. He was passionate about success, which led him to do things in a very unique fashion. His passion was towards life, his performance, detailing, and delivering world class music to his fans.

His passion ignited a series of other traits which resulted in his becoming a global icon of music. His passion gave way to innovation. He made a mark in singing, dancing, and even marketing. That kind of creation and innovation set him apart from the masses as he

Desire is the starting point of all achievement, not a hope, not a wish, but a keen pulsating desire, which triggers traits within and transcends everything around.

—Napoleon Hill

evolved from good to great. He was different and dimensional, whether it was wearing just one glove when the rest of the world was wearing two. His shows included an integrated texture of sights, themes and sounds, with almost unimaginable dance moves, complex lighting design, and countless imaginative costume changes. You could sense his deep involvement in every aspect, from designing of the lighting and pyrotechnics, the selection of dancers, direction of performance, and the way of playing music. He intimately knew how he wanted to present himself to the world. Each of his move captured Michael's intensity and devotion to every aspect of the show.

Through his passion for purpose he became a source of continuously emanating energy. Highly energetic himself, he had the capacity to energise others all the time. Two things that maximised his chance of success were his preparation and execution.

He brought changes in his style and performance at regular interval to avoid monotony. He maintained that element of surprise which renewed excitement and kept people engaged. He was diverse in thinking and risked new roles to avoid monotony that steal our excitement and passion for life.

Michael approached everything with passion for purpose of satisfying his fans, to fulfil their dreams, to appear his very best before them and he was intensely focussed on this goal. He seemed to understand the benefits he offered his audience through entertainment. Apart from exceptional talent he had exceptional ability to focus and make the most of time. The more general point is that everyone should have a daily purpose and goal. By focussing on that goal, whether it may be to push yourself further on the daily exercise regime or give a passer by a smile, it makes the day much easier and productive. It helps to prevent getting caught up on the small, negative things, like a traffic jam, and focus on the things that are really important to you, things that make you feel important. Wake up every day with passion for your purpose and a desire to achieve excellence.

He was performance and perfection in motion. He studied, researched, and rehearsed endlessly. The desire to learn

www.universalhunt.com

more with an undying inquisitiveness propelled him to explore, discover, and grow. His passion kept him committed for his life. His passion forced him to dream big. He referred to Michelangelo's wisdom in stating that the creator must die but his works will live on... Mission Accomplished!

Following your passion gives you so much enjoyment that it motivates you to give 100% to your interests. It adds unique value to your customers, friends and family, which is most meaningful.

COMMUNICATION

A leader is a passionate communicator with the capacity to drive his vision through barriers of time, place and reality; making others see, feel and experience a situation which at times never existed in the past, nor appears possible in future.

Every leader is an excellent communicator. He has tremendous capacity to communicate his vision, concepts and understanding of situations to others. Through a leader's powerful art of communication, people understand a situation clearly and have no scope of getting confused. Information communicated by a leader normally does not get distorted. Strong communication doesn't mean strong command over multiple languages. Leaders are highly expressive. They are able to deliver the message in the desired format. For example, a good

The language of leadership is the art of communication.

political leader during any gathering conveys his message, vision, goals very effectively, winning many followers. Similarly singers have an amazing fan following for they effectively communicate the language of emotions through their songs. By displaying their capacity to enable you to visualise today what is likely to exist in future, leaders create a strong faith in the minds of their followers and create genuine fans that follow them in executing various tasks.

In order to ensure best communication, several things are to be taken care of:

- Most important of these is content or topic which touches the heart, mind and soul of every addressee. Leaders are good at understanding what people want to hear, what is popular or what is the pressing issue.

- Second most important is the usage of language. Many have multilingual skills. It is best when you address the people in the language of their choice. Though you may have better command over some other language but it is always important to address the recipients in the language which helps you in relating with them.

- Even more important than language is the tone. Leaders know when to be gentle, when to be harsh, when to demand, and when to request. Leaders are best at twisting the tone depending on the situation and mood of the crowd. For this one has to be excellent at feeling and sensing the mood of the masses.

- Leaders have excellent listening and analytical capacity which makes them judge reactions of a crowd. Through this they adjust their own tone to the tone of recipients keeping the end result in mind.

- Timing, duration and venue of communication - all are equally important keeping the purpose and addressee in mind. Sometimes leaders purposely choose odd hours or some historic place or a secret place to enhance the attention and convey the importance. Duration of speech is equally important. It should not be too short that the message is incomplete nor it should be too long during which people either get bored or develop suspicion for the speaker and try to find if there could be any personal interest behind all those talks. Many a time they also use other leaders or association to correlate their cause or create perception of an image which is acceptable to people.

To make an effective connection you have to use the full range of your communication channels. As per a research, out of your total communication, words count for a mere 7%, tone of voice 38%, and body language for the remaining 55%.

Sometimes I used to wonder what makes leaders best communicators or why they are able to deliver with so much passion. There are so many people who may have better command over language and have no stage fear; still they can't be compared to the way a leader delivers and sways the crowd. Leaders are highly passionate about achievement of the goal and extremely confident of the purpose for achieving the goal. Hence the rhythm and passion with which they communicate makes you believe them. A leader's belief in his vision sparks the highest level of confidence which makes others believe in him. Most of the time when people listen to you, more than language their focus is on confidence, passion, attachment, clarity of purpose, and ultimate vision of the leader.

Great Communicators are made and not necessarily born that way. Communication improves with conscious and continuous practise. Many a time it is wrongly assumed that leaders, who are great communicators, were born with the natural talent of oration since childhood. On the contrary, Ronald Reagan was trained by some of the best acting coaches in the world and consistently worked on his timing and delivery. Clinton, who had closely studied the speeches and communication styles of John F Kennedy and Martin Luther King, worked intensely on his communication skills undergoing both neuro-linguistic programming and body language training. The results of this leadership communication coaching are evident to all and were key factors in Clinton's ability to maintain his popularity throughout the various storms he encountered during his presidency. Like Reagan and Clinton, Obama is reputed to have worked hard on improving his public speaking abilities. You only need to see some earlier film footage of Obama speaking, to trace the significant improvement in his performance.

Unless a leader connects with people, he will fail to achieve his true leadership potential. There is a need for establishing a connection that leaves the other people feeling that they matter, even in some small way. A leader must connect with people on an emotional level, as that is where they can have the greatest impact and influence. People form opinions and make decisions based on their emotions. First, people listen to their emotional guidance system, then they justify with reasons, and rationalise. Bill Clinton is very effective at engaging people by making them feel that they matter. In the early years of his presidency, Clinton speaking to members of the public, often used the phrase, "I feel your pain". Through the effective use of body language, eye contact, smiles, and listening skills, Clinton appears to radiate a form of "feel good" energy which is described as "charisma".

If you observe, Barack Obama has tremendous skill to connect with the audience and sense the prevailing mood. He delivers his speeches with confidence and self-belief. He seems to be very comfortable with the audience. He listens to every question from the audience and gives a very personable response. A good communicator needs to foremost make the listeners believe in his vision. In this case, Barack Obama was successful in making the entire America believe in his message of "change". It is not only enough to know your facts but it is paramount that you deliver them while holding the attention of the audience.

Let us understand through some examples as to what helps in developing strong communication skills that ultimately adds to leadership traits. Here I have picked examples of world class communicators and global leaders. This will lend a new perspective to our understanding of the importance of communication.

Winston Churchill:

Sir Winston Churchill (30 November 1874 – 24 January 1965) was a British politician known chiefly for his leadership of the United Kingdom during World War II. Churchill created a strong position for himself by his stimulating, systematic and well planned communication techniques. Widely regarded as one of the great wartime leaders, he served as Prime Minister from 1940 to 1945 and again from 1951 to 1955. A noted statesman and orator, Churchill was also an officer in the British Army, a historian, writer and artist. He is the only British Prime Minister to have received the Nobel Prize in Literature till date, and the first person to be recognised as an honorary citizen of the United States.

Churchill's example reflects that it is not necessary to be a good communicator from the beginning. It is not a problem if one does not have communication strength as a natural gift. It can very well be developed over a period of time. Winston Churchill was a master communicator. It perhaps goes without saying that the trait of communication is an essential aspect of almost every task. Leadership is about working productively with others, and this cannot be achieved without the ability to communicate. Churchill worked hard at drafting his key note speeches to the nation or House of Commons. Though not a born orator he was a perfectionist and would craft, rehearse and rework, long into the night. He was never at loss of words – and produced an enormous output of memos, directives and reports. As a Prime Minister, he decided that every order, proposal, suggestion or instruction would be in writing. He communicated to his senior staff and all his private office that "Let it be clearly understood, that all directions emanating from me are made in writing, or should be immediately afterwards confirmed in writing, and that I do not accept any responsibility for matters relating to national defence, on which I am alleged to have given directions, unless they are given in writing." This had two key effects, it minimised the disorder and acted as a steadying influence on Winston's impulsive nature – forcing him to think before suggesting a course of action.

Language used by Churchill in his speeches was impressive

and classy. Each speech unfolded his argument carefully; with wonderful sweeping turns of phrase delivering impressive, clear, and convincing messages that appealed to both the heart and the head of the listeners. He had a marvellous ability to simplify and streamline complex issues and effectively give spin-free fluent executive summaries to the nation. He could summarise the big picture in the simplest fashion for the easy understanding of common men.

Churchill also focussed on communication systems. Immediately after he became the Prime Minister, Churchill radically reorganised the communication systems between the politicians and the heads of the three military services. As part of this, Churchill created and headed the Ministry of Defence. This avoided some of the problems of the First World War when communication between the army and the navy was frequently an issue. Also reporting to the Ministry of Defence were key planning and intelligence staff. Other boards such as Production Council, Raw Materials Board, Battle of the Atlantic Committee, Import Executive, etc., were set up as their need arose. Each board had a high degree of Churchill's input. All of this gave Churchill enormous access to all the key information that people needed to run a country in wartime.

To emerge out as an effective communicator, Churchill gave maximum adherence to personal organisation. The workload of any peacetime Prime Minister is prodigious and that of a wartime leader must be tenfold greater. Therefore, it was necessary for Churchill to have an effective private office to support him. At the core of this team were his private secretaries who worked at his side all days of the week. This team got to know Winston better than all his closest friends and family, and were able to interpret at the merest signal. They were able to retrieve any relevant document or person as per the requirement and they managed his diary and appointments irrespective of where Churchill was in the world. This all communication made him a successful wartime leader.

Churchill was a great leader and orator. He personally visited factories, gun batteries, bomb damaged streets, etc. and gave wonderful boosts to the morale of the people working there. He would pose with them to give wonderful photo opportunities for the next day's newspapers and newsreels. His trademarks: Bowker hat, spotted bowties, cigar and V-sign made him vastly memorable. Winston carried out personal meetings, and coined the idea of summits. He travelled extensively to meet and inspire people of USA, Canada, Malta, Casablanca, Normandy, Moscow, Tehran, Yalta, Rhineland, African desert, etc. Leaving aside the honour of a grand state funeral, Churchill received a wide range of awards and honours. Churchill received the Nobel Prize in Literature in 1953 for his numerous published works, especially the six-volume set-*The Second World War*. In a 2002 BBC poll of the "100 Greatest Britons", he was proclaimed "The Greatest of Them All" based on approximately a million votes from BBC viewers. Churchill was also rated as one of the most influential leaders in history by the *Time*. Churchill College, Cambridge was founded in 1958 on his behalf.

It is very rightly said leaders can never be compared. Each has his own style, charisma and different blend of basic traits which emerge out in the form of a unique persona that simply inspires people to follow them. They sense the need and put things in motion for generations to come. One such leader and one of the greatest communicators who sensed the need for equality and put the movement for civil rights in motion was Martin Luther King Jr.

Martin Luther King Jr.:

Martin Luther King Jr. (15 January 1929 – 4 April 1968) was an American clergyman, who later turned into an activist by prominently leading the African American civil rights movement. He became the human rights icon for his relentless efforts in securing progress on civil rights in the United States. Very early in his life he became a civil rights activist. He led the 1955 Montgomery Bus Boycott and helped found the Southern Christian Leadership Conference in 1957, serving as its first president. King's efforts led to the 1963 March on Washington, where he raised public consciousness of the civil rights movement and established himself as one of the greatest orators in U.S. history by delivering his "I Have a Dream" speech.

In 1964, he became the youngest person to receive the Nobel Peace Prize for his prominent contribution in ending racial segregation and racial discrimination through civil disobedience and other non-violent methods. By early 1968, he had refocused his efforts on ending poverty and the Vietnam War through a religious perspective. King was assassinated on 4 April 1968, in Memphis, Tennessee. He was posthumously awarded the Presidential Medal of Freedom in 1977 and Congressional Gold Medal in 2004. Martin Luther King, Jr. Day was established as a national holiday in the U.S. in 1986.

His splendid "I Have A Dream" speech, which he delivered from the steps of the Lincoln Memorial, galvanised people of all races, and created an unprecedented bipartisan coalition for anti-racist legislation. His move for racial justice and an integrated society took a concrete shape for Americans in the form of the US Declaration of Independence. His words helped people in understanding the social and political upheaval of the time and gave the nation a vocabulary to express what was happening. The key message of his speech was that all people are created equal. He argued passionately and powerfully in favour of it.

What made his speech so stimulating and influencing? Factors that made his speech so soulful were:

- Remarkable emotion of King's delivery in terms of both voice and body.

- Apt location of delivery, which was on the steps of the memorial to the President who defeated southern states over the issue of slavery.

- Perfect timing, mood of the day, a sense of perpetuated slavery among black people, and the gradual realisation of a sense of guilt among white people.

Speaker's emotions, his location, and timing of delivery of speech are the right formula for success. Right place and timing often helps you in aligning the people emotionally to the tune at which they can connect to you summarily.

It wasn't that King was a great orator or a literary whiz or had sculptured impressive physique. But his intense passion in delivery and connection with people through trust made people connect with him. This passion and trustworthiness was as a result of sheer display of Courage, Conviction, Clarity, Credibility and Wisdom. He courageously spoke against the status quo and challenged conventional wisdom without a tinge of fear. With deep conviction in his ideology and strong belief in himself, he wonderfully expressed the suppressed viewpoint of millions. His message was clear and concise, simplified for the easy understanding of common man. His inclusive vision encompassed not only the dream of every American African but the dream of every human who believed in equality and independence. He had mastered the skill to defend his ideas effectively. These attributes are essential, not only for speaking in front of hundreds of people, but also for writing a report to your boss, and for running a board meeting. They help a speaker or writer in getting his point across effectively.

Conventionally, successful communication demands preparation. The communication should be world class. Each mail you write, message you send, "thank you" note you give, book you write, word you speak, gesture you make, expressions you give should be world class. Practising brings perfection. Whatever you do; try to do it in a world class manner. Even when you may be talking to a group of three people, prepare and speak as if you are on air before one million people. Prepare like Shakira or Madonna or Michael Jackson when on stage before a crowd of thousands. Make sure you are noticed and judged each time. You should simply impress anyone and everyone who comes in your direct or indirect contact. King's speech was well researched and practised. In preparation, he is said to have studied the *Bible*, The Gettysburg Address and the US Declaration of Independence and he alluded to all three in his address.

King tuned and retuned his voice modulations. Initially, when he sensed that he was not reaching his audience as effectively as expected, he began speaking spontaneously speaking from the heart. The result was electrifying. It's well known that King delivered most of the "I Have a Dream" speech without any notes and that he improvised much of it on the spot. We usually see King in thirty second clips of him at the climax of his speeches; we tend to think of him as a very forceful and passionate speaker. Clearly, he was that, but he was more than that. When you listen to his complete speeches, you'd observe that he almost always started out at a slow, and eventually increased his pace and volume as he drew the audience in. This is how one can use modulation to bring your audience along when you speak.

He made effective use of repetition. We all know his famous

sentence "I have a dream" because he repeated it so often and people could relate to what he said.

I have a dream ... that one day this nation will rise up and live out the true meaning its creed. I have a dream ... that one day on the red hills of Georgia the sons of former slaves and the sons of former slave owners will be able to sit down together at the table of brotherhood. I have a dream ... that one day even the State of Mississippi ... will be transformed into an oasis of freedom and justice. I have a dream... that my four little children will one day live in a nation where they will not be judged by the colour of their skin but by the content of their character. I have a dream today.

This kind of refrain of "I have a dream" enabled him to clearly make his main point and also make the audience connect with it and remember it till many years later.

Know your audience well. Don't restrict yourself to present context; understand them in historic and futuristic context. King quoted Biblical phrases and national songs well-known to his listeners. Then he elaborated upon those references and made them relevant to his theme of racial equality and harmony. King was a master in establishing the historical context for his message. He regularly started with stories from the Old Testament and modern history to make the point that the people in his movement were part of the broad sweep of history. That could relate audience with a sense of mission.

Most important of all, an aspiring leader should clarify his vision and purpose of life to all involved. When listeners find common goals, connect is established and ground is set enhancing the receptivity. King let his audience know exactly what he stood for, leaving no doubt about topic, and there by developing connect with his audience. They drew their energy from each other and that connection made the event more than a speech making it an experience that moved people to act. You must have a cause to be a great leader and communicator.

His speech was a masterpiece, a passionate emotional sermon, carved out of the language and spirit of democracy.

SELF-DISCIPLINE

The quality of a leader is reflected in the
standards he sets for himself.

When we say discipline, it means self discipline and must not be misinterpreted as infusing discipline in others. If one is not willing to be disciplined from within, external factors can't generate discipline for long. If it is developed out of fear or pressure, a person ends up suppressing certain needs, and the desire for those suppressed needs keeps building over a period of time. As soon as the external control is removed, he starts behaving in the direction of fulfilment of suppressed needs.

Discipline should be developed by enriching yourself with right knowledge and possible benefits/consequences of actions.

Discipline means learning self control, recognising acceptable limits, and learning where to stop, and how to stop. Discipline is the instant willingness and obedience to self orders, respect for self and self reliance even in teamwork. It is the ability to do the right thing even when no one is watching. Discipline means being conscious of the larger purpose of life while doing the smallest action.

Leadership is doing what is RIGHT when no one is watching.

A good leader has the discipline to work towards his or her vision single-mindedly, as well as to direct his or her actions and those of the team towards the goal. With discipline, leaders are able to overcome every possible limitation in achieving their vision. If you dream as big as you can dream, and follow it with discipline, anything is possible.

Leaders are basically disciplined people with highly disciplined thoughts and actions. They are self-controlled in almost all circumstances.

Disciplined behaviour is display of basic physical,

intellectual, emotional and even spiritual fitness. One needs to train himself to get aligned on all these fronts. Unless you are yourself fit, you have no right to lead people in any direction. Because leadership is a responsible task where people try to imitate your moves, actions, lifestyle; a role model has to be disciplined in whatever he does. He has to be perfect. He must expect perfection out of himself because people expect him to be a superstar if he is supposed to be a role model as a leader.

Because leaders are disciplined by nature, they are disciplined even in the pursuit of their goals and do not deviate from the same until they achieve them. Their strong sense of purpose, clarity of thought, clear vision, and irrefutable passion to achieve everything that is planned to achieve, keeps them highly motivated, and hence completely focussed.

They are experts in multitasking but never deviate from basic ethics or discipline. They never change the larger goal. I have seen people wanting to do many things out of influence of so many people they come across and by the time they come close to success they change the goal. They neither achieve success in anything taken up and at the same time end up wasting resources, thereby feeling lost and de-motivated.

Disciplined person, once clear about purpose, doesn't give up until he achieves the goal. Even if he starts doing something parallel, it would ultimately have some link to the larger goal or he would have planned resources for the same. He would not take up anything at the cost of something already going on. He would though try multiple ways but would not give up any particular method without going deep or far. Their high degree of sensitivity, understanding and intelligence enables them to take most appropriate judgement on how much is enough, or how much more effort is required to attain perfection. They probe everything and get to the depth of the situation. They dissect every situation into multiple cases and analyse, and solve each, one by one, and achieve proper result.

They are also patient in nature. Do not confuse patient behaviour with being lazy. Leaders do not have time, they always have sense of urgency but they do not take any action in haste. They are able to calculate beforehand the intensity of the task and hence the time it would likely take. They calculate the time each task should be given before making any change in the means or method to achieve the same. Their good judgemental capacity adds to their disciplined nature.

They think and act disciplined which enhances their capacity to work on minute details in a short time span. They think of every possible permutation and combination within the focussed area, hence visualising and evaluating likely probabilities of outcome, discarding methods leading to negative outcomes and following methods leading to exact desired outcomes.

They are able to foresee results before they start because they do not allow their brain to clutter with unwanted thoughts and at the same time develop a capacity to handle multiple desirable disciplined thoughts.

Their thoughts being highly disciplined and controlled result in well planned actions. They do not normally act on anything which goes out of control. Even when they delegate, they delegate to right people. They do not act impulsive or repelling. They continue to impress people around and increasing their followers who are charmed by their confidence and calmness.

Disciplined thoughts and actions result into desired outcomes, which enhance a leader's confidence and faith in being disciplined and behaving disciplined. This makes a cyclic impact on their behaviour adding more discipline to their thoughts and actions making them sharper, faster and accurate.

Sometimes people think that being disciplined might kill innovation or creativity but they should understand that discipline breeds immense creativity. This is why leaders are deemed as the most creative thinkers. One needs to be disciplined and consistent even to innovate. Leaders are good at setting systems and processes for desired action and follow them religiously. One has to infuse discipline even in creativity because to remain creative one needs to constantly try multiple permutations-combinations in a disciplined fashion without making their actions repeated or monotonous. Even deciding to be non repetitive requires discipline.

> "Insanity is doing the same thing over and over again and expecting different results."
>
> —Albert Einstein

In order to develop discipline as a habit, we need not do something very big. It begins with small things, especially time discipline and then it becomes a habit. It is best if infused at childhood level. Acquiring discipline of time puts everything in motion. Start with simple things like waking up on time, eating on time, reaching school or college or office in time. I have seen most people fail to reach office or for meeting or even for interview in time. Most interviewers also fail to meet interviewee at planned time. Lack of

> "You will find the key to success under the alarm clock."
>
> —Benjamin Franklin

The greater control you exercise over your time, the greater freedom you will experience in your life.

planning, carelessness, whatever you may call it, but it is undisciplined behaviour. It simply shows that they lack self control and self respect.

Spend at least three to six hours on sports or at gym per week. If you can't take care of your health, I am sure you can't show discipline for any other goal you have set. If you are not fit, not only you would fail to lead but even if you are successful in life, you would not be able to enjoy life the way you would have otherwise done. Learn to be careful about yourself; people watch, analyse and judge you, though they may not reveal their judgement about you. Once you develop the habit of being disciplined in every action, you tend to follow the same degree of discipline even in perusing larger goals and purposes of life.

In most of the cases people are not disciplined because they do not have any goal to pursue. They do not have any strong passion for purpose. They do things for the sake of doing. They are working on those goals which are set for them by others. They go to office because they have a job, not necessarily to build a career or make a difference in the society.

Set goals for yourself. Please do not set very large or vague goals which are difficult to measure. In case your goal is too large then you must learn to break it down into smaller measurable goals. Define actions required to achieve these goals. Measure and monitor these actions. Put them on paper and you shall see the difference. Leadership traits are interlinked and complementary. One triggers another. Envisioning, decisiveness and passion act as supports in being disciplined.

Many of us have different goals. You might have a goal to become a doctor or artist or join the best management school, or to become a supermodel or superstar or a CEO. Just remember your goal every moment. It is very important to have goals because if you won't keep goals you would never experience sense of achievement or fulfilment or even growth. Through discipline, people can overcome major limitations in life.

Let's assume that the goal is to become CEO after five years. One needs to be very clear that each year would be of 365 days and each day of twenty-four hours and each hour of sixty minutes and each minute of sixty seconds. That means whatever action you take *You can be lucky enough for an overnight success only after years of hard work in a disciplined fashion.* every second will either bring you closer to or away from your set goal. If you keep your long term goal in mind, then you will perform every action keeping the final result in mind. This way you would take the right desired action in the direction of your goal. One needs to work every second for years in a disciplined fashion to achieve overnight success.

Set a vision/purpose. Break it down into smaller goals, milestones, list out actions linked to each milestone, measure and monitor your actions, and take corrective steps on actions if a goal is not achieved. Once your goal is achieved, move to the next goal until the desired larger purpose/ vision is fulfilled. Follow this process in a systemic fashion *"Leaders aren't born, they are made. And they are made just like anything else, through hard work. And that's the price we'll have to pay to achieve that goal, or any goal."*

—Vincent Lombardi

without deviating from the set path or altering the purpose. Discipline sets into your actions, making this as a natural trait and you would start following this pattern in everything that you decide to pursue, until you achieve a larger purpose of life, experience growth and fulfilment.

Let's understand this trait through two special leaders in the field of sports. Wilma Rudolph suffered from polio at the age of four, but at the age of twenty two won three Olympic medals and became a champion in her field. Michael Phelps, who suffered from ADHD disorder at the age of nine, emerged out to be a winner of multiple gold medals and was tagged as the Greatest Olympian.

Wilma Rudolph:

When Wilma Rudolph was four years old, she had polio that made her crippled and she was unable to walk. Moreover, she belonged to a large family with poor financial conditions. She was the 20th child among twenty-two children of her parents. Her father was a railroad porter and her mother was a maid.

The doctors had said she would never be able to walk. Her mother took her every week to a hospital to receive therapy. Doctors recommended giving Wilma a massage every day on her legs. By the age of eight, she started walking with a leg brace. After that, she used a high-topped shoe to support her foot, and started playing basketball with her brothers every day. Three years later, Wilma was able to walk without any support or special shoes.

A track coach encouraged her to start running and this set her rolling with the training in a much disciplined fashion. During her senior year in high school, she qualified for the 1956 Olympics in Melbourne, Australia. She won a bronze medal in the women's 400-metre relay. In 1959, she qualified for the 1960 Olympic Games in Rome by setting a world record in the 200-metre race. At the Olympics that year, she won three gold medals; for the 100-metre race, 200-metre race and 400-metre relay!

She retired from running when she was just twenty-two years old and went on to coach women's track teams and encourage young people. Wilma thought God had a greater purpose for her than to win three gold medals. She started the Wilma Rudolph Foundation to help children learn about discipline and hard work.

Michael Phelps:

In the summer of 2008, the world found a new hero in a six foot four inch swimmer, Michael Phelps. Michael was the youngest of three children in his family. While he was growing up, he was tall and lanky. At the age of nine he was diagnosed with ADHD, attention deficit hyperactivity disorder. He couldn't sit still or concentrate, and was always on the move. A teacher told his mother that he would never be able to focus. His performance in school was also below average.

When he was young, he developed interest in sports like baseball, soccer and swimming. By the time he was eleven, he found his niche and concentrated on swimming.

He made his first Olympic team in Sydney, Australia in the 200 butterfly race in the year 2000 when he was just fifteen years old. In 2004, at the Athens Olympics he won six gold medals and two bronze medals. At the 2007 world championships in Melbourne, he won seven gold medals. In 2008 Olympics in Beijing, he won eight gold medals!

Michael's third grade teacher wrote a letter to his mother telling how proud she was of him. She said perhaps it was never the focus he had lacked, but, rather, a goal worthy of his focus.

Phelps follows a disciplined schedule. He swims seven days a week, two to five hours a day. His life revolves around swimming, sleeping, and eating. Swimming burns a lot of calories; hence he consumes 8,000-12,000 calories a day, five times as much as the average man eats. He has designed his complete lifestyle around his goal in a much disciplined fashion.

Both these examples simply indicate that with discipline and focus you can even overcome natural hurdles. These people are heroes/leaders in their fields. They are champions of success. The most valuable gift a leader can give is a good example. A person doing his or her best becomes a natural leader, just by example.

CAPACITY to GIVE-UP POWER and EMPOWER

Leader is one who makes you feel bigger when you are with him.

A leader is never hungry for power, he is hungry for purpose. Leaders gain power in the process of achieving the purpose. They never assume power to achieve the purpose. Hence, even when they have to give up power they don't actually face any difficulty because they psychologically never had it. While giving up power what they simply transfer is authority and responsibility of actions, yet keeping themselves overall responsible. They indeed never get away from responsibility. They always remain powerful by taking responsibility for larger acts likely to be performed in the near future.

Management works in the system; leadership works on the system.

In the context of business world, the goal of many managers is to get people to think more highly of the manager but they fail to realise that the goal of a great leader is to help people to think more highly of themselves. A good leader takes a little more than his share of the blame, a little less than his share of the credit. There's no limit to what can be accomplished if you don't care who gets the credit.

Do the hard jobs first. The easy jobs will take care of themselves.

Capacity to give up power and empower is a process of moving up the ladder. You can't hold on to the ladder that you are climbing. Leaders normally do not stay still. They mean growth for which they constantly need to move up the ladder of success. They need to complete one task, give that up once systems are set and move on to the next level. In order to attain a large vision, leaders define certain goals. Each goal is related to a project or an activity. When they start afresh, it is an unknown territory at each step which requires understanding, defining of systems and processes and setting standards. By the time these are attained, leaders gain tremendous power purely out of maximum knowledge gained in the process, having first mover advantage, having recruited people for that activity which naturally makes him a parent and an accepted leader and last but not the least having trained people for that activity. A leader's goal is not to fulfil this activity or hang on to this alone, but to move on to a higher level of activity, for which he gives up the current activity or makes himself free of current operations, without affecting set systems. It is not only important for a leader to give up power but also essential to empower others who can do the tasks in his absence and the handover is smooth.

We must understand that this process is a step beyond delegation. In case of delegation, one just has to give up and people are ready to take the process further, whereas in the case of empowering, one needs to create a situation by providing relevant training and creating importance for the immediate next person in the minds of other team members in the

The job of a leader is to produce more leaders, not followers; they are just by- product of the effort.

organization, who were looking at you as a leader. You need to create stars out of people before they are mentally ready to become stars. Leaders are kingmakers. As a leader, one needs to initiate this exercise from the beginning otherwise when there is a time to move on, you may not have people enabled to take care or the team may not be mentally prepared to accept the next leader. Here one needs to have a two prong strategy. One not only has to make/guide/prepare the next leader but one also has to sell the next leader to others who have been looking at you as a leader. This all needs to be done so that you are free to pursuit a larger goal.

True leaders know it best, when to give up power or fame. Importance of their vision and values in their own eyes is so strong that when they feel that their personal want or love for being a leader comes in the way, they are ready to give up that and emerge out to be stronger because they end up adding more people who appreciate their commitment to the purpose beyond their personal gain.

Leaders have the capacity to empower others, which as a result of good relationship, is at the heart of effective leaders. They embody a deeply caring approach to people, seeing them as their greatest assets.

Leaders do not hesitate to give credit where it is due. A magnanimous leader ensures that credit for various successes is spread as widely as possible throughout the company or institution or group. Conversely, a good leader takes personal responsibility for failures. This sort of reverse magnanimity helps other people feel good about themselves and draws the team closer together. To spread the fame and take the blame is a hallmark of effective leadership.

A good leader inspires men to have confidence in him; a great leader inspires them to have confidence in themselves.

The art of giving up is very important. Normally leaders give up a task once they find the right person who can take care of the current task so that they can move to higher level of tasks. They never leave a task unfinished but transfer their powers to the next best person. It is the responsibility of a leader to provide opportunity, and the responsibility of individuals to contribute.

The best leader is the one who has sense enough to pick good men to do what he wants done, and self-restraint to keep from meddling with them while they do it.

A man will not be a great leader if he wants to do it all himself and get all the credit for it. If one cannot give powers then he would keep himself occupied even while doing even the smallest of the tasks, feel busy and remain involved in tasks which may not remain important over a period of time due to the changing needs. Whereas what is essential for a leader is to understand a task,

> "My grandfather once told me that there were two kinds of people: those who do the work and those who take the credit. He told me to try to be in the first group. There is much less competition."
>
> —*Indira Gandhi*

set up systems and processes, find the right person who can share same perspective in sync with the leader, and move on to find the next level of challenge, set systems again at the next level, find again the next best person and move on.

People in the second line to leader normally move along with leader taking up the tasks transferred by him so that he can be allowed to explore a new territory. They in turn develop the next best breed of leaders. It is nothing but transfer of leadership trait.

Leaders always create a "core" team, a team of likeminded people who can substitute the leader for ongoing activity over a period of time. They train them, share vision and partner them in terms of professional authority and responsibility. They also ensure that these people gel well with each other and function as a team. It is a process of team creation which reflects empowerment. A leader normally may be the face of the team or organisation, but there is a core team which acts as mind, body and soul. If a leader does not have the capacity to develop core team, then he cannot move on. He can never relieve himself of ongoing tasks, and can't take new challenges. He must initiate this activity from day one at the time of setting vision. If there is any task that you are currently performing cannot be performed by one more person in your team, you are a failure as a leader. It doesn't mean that all tasks that you do need to be performed by someone, but can be managed collectively. Whenever you initiate any activity you must be clear to prepare at least a few people to hand over the same before you take a leap at the next level. Reason for preparing more than one person is that there are always chances of discontinuity of people from task and if that doesn't happen there is scope for doubling up the scale, for more growth.

Every person in the core team needs to have good leadership skills, vision alignment and technical knowhow to execute the tasks assigned by the leader. The member of the core team should eventually shoulder 100% responsibility allowing the leader to move on to explore unchartered territory. These people are extremely good at execution.

If you want to give up power it is more important that you have extremely strong trusted followers who have the capacity and willingness to manage what you have transferred. Strong sense of understanding, ownership and vision alignment results into development of such followers.

Followers are outcome of Leaders' efforts to develop more leaders.

You can observe this phenomenon happening with every leader around you, be it in case of a business leader, political leader, religious leader, or social leader. There would usually be around five strong "leaders in making" who would be a leader's core team members whose names would always be in circulation for handling tasks currently managed by the leader. Those people would all be of almost equal capacity and commitment.

A leader by definition is a person who is capable of setting up successful institution beyond his personal influence. Things must run smoothly even after he has given up the task to move to the next one. Succession planning is most important.

If a person has become a leader with smaller vision or hunger for power or fame, then his empire/ organisation would thrive till he is in command, but after he gives up or dies, the empire collapses, the ideology vanishes and there is no single strong follower who can take it from there. Try to empower, rather than controlling people who look up to you for leadership. Leadership is elevating a person's vision beyond his independent capacity to increase his performance standards and craft his personality beyond his personal limitations.

"It is better to lead from behind and put others in front, especially while celebrating victory. You should take the front line when there is danger. It is then that people will appreciate your leadership."

—Nelson Mandela

A leader is a person who is capable of creating leaders consciously. He does not let his followers remain mere followers for life. He transforms them into leaders. A leader's conscious effort is always in creating leaders by finding the right replacement. Practically there is no replacement for a leader; he is only replaced so that he can be made free for something higher.

Leaders have a vision beyond their life. The very scale and size of their vision makes them naturally think beyond one life so it is compulsive to institutionalise the system and make it independent of individual capacity and develop more leaders to achieve the vision in duration less than the lifetime of the visionary.

A man who wants to lead the orchestra must turn his back on the crowd.

Leaders promote a partnership approach and create a shared sense of vision along with others. They exhibit greater respect for others and carefully develop team spirit and team learning. They build a sense of shared vision and partnership.

Normally people do not give up power and they do not empower others due to fear of being side-tracked, fear of losing job, fear of losing importance that they currently enjoy being in a decision-making authoritative situation where others are perceptually dependent on them. The reason behind this fear is the lack of knowledge. Normally such people after attaining a certain stage or success feel contented and revel in the comfort of the environment, where all the systems are set. This way they end up being a bottle neck in the system for growth. If the leader does not move on and tries to stick around for longer time despite systems being set, then the people who follow him or look up to him will fail to get room for growth. Hence they would either revolt or move in the search of a new leader or organisation where there is room for personal growth. It is very important for every leader to understand that he is like a growth engine. People follow him because of

"To lead people, walk behind them... As for the best leaders, the people do not notice their existence. The next best, the people honour and praise. The next, the people fear; and the next, the people hate. When the best leader's work is done the people say, 'we did it ourselves."

—Lao Tzu

one simple reason, growth. If he cannot give growth to others he would no longer remain a leader. People would simply leave him. Remember one thing; no one has ever suffered because of strong and effective subordinate!

A leader, unlike normal persons, does not fear competition because he is always in the search of more and higher knowledge. He is always ready to take risk of venturing into unknown territory for the elevation of his goals, and for fulfilment of his vision. Hence he easily gives up power without being threatened about being replaced. Rather he is always in a hurry to be replaced at his own will and time for a particular task so that he can carry out other activities which are required to achieve higher level of new tasks.

"I have three precious things which I hold fast and prize. The first is gentleness; the second is frugality; the third is humility, which keeps me from putting myself before others. Be gentle and you can be bold; be frugal and you can be liberal; avoid putting yourself before others and you can become a leader among men."

—Lao-Tzu

The most gifted athletes rarely make good coaches. Nor does the best teacher necessarily make the best head of the department. It is critical to distinguish between the skill of performance and the skill of leading the performance, the two being entirely different skills. It's also important to determine whether a best performer is capable of learning leadership. The natural leader will stand out.

Leadership is the ability to inspire vision and strength within people through empowerment. The very soul of leadership is a leader's commitment to make people grow and progress. This is accomplished when leaders use their words to convey faith, hope and love to their followers. Conversely, when leaders communicate fear, hostility, jealousy and doubt to people, the confidence, morale, and productivity of followers plummet. Leaders must learn how to use communication to strengthen their team mates, and not scare, insult, or tear them down.

I have given so many examples of leaders till now. When you come across any situation and you are short of options, just think what these leaders would have done. How Gandhi or Mandela would have reacted in a situation like this and by and large you would get the right solution. Choose your role models right. Follow Madonna for innovation and Michael Jackson for passion, Gandhi and Mandela for envisioning and compassion. There are certain "golden rules" we must follow to speed up the process of empowerment and avoid any negative influence of any action on the team.

As a leader, you have no right to comment on anyone's negativity or weakness in front of others. By doing so, you eventually lose self-respect and respect amongst colleagues. Do not comment on your colleague or your boss, irrespective of any situation you are into. Do not display such behaviour after your appraisal which may not be in alignment with your expectation and never after you have resigned from organization. Neither in the coffee break with colleagues, nor with your friends who may or may not have anything to do with your organisation. If you have problem with someone or if you genuinely wish to give feedback to someone, keep the courage to talk to that person looking in his eyes with the aim of genuine advice. Even when you are advising a

Leadership should be more participative than directive, more enabling than performing.

colleague or a subordinate make sure you do not try to criticise him or make fun or be harsh to him. Your intention should be to improve him. Do not tell him only what is wrong but emphasise on the right. A leader must train himself to respond to people in a positive and motivating manner. Negativity only produces more negative energy. Never react emotionally. Exercise self-control and act with grace. Express how much you care for your teammates and never leave a chance to praise them for their accomplishments.

Let us understand how a leader can follow a systematic process of empowering people through positive communication. Secret lies in transparent, positive and empathetic communication. When you assume a position of a leader you need to be really empathetic to others, including your seniors, subordinates, and peers. A basic need amongst all people is the desire to be accepted by their equals, superiors as well as subordinates. This will result in empowered and energised teammates who know their leaders believe in them. Leaders must be intentional about their communication, which should make others feel important and accepted. When your team gives an excellent performance on a task, do not let it go unnoticed; instead reward them with public praise, awards and promotions. When people do things right, let them know you care. Giving people attention helps in their empowerment and progress. Make it a mission to take the spotlight off yourself and place it onto your people. Communicate to them how much they mean to you and how valuable their contribution is for the success and sustainability of the organisation. See your followers as partners. Remember that a leader's success will always be measured by the growth and development of his people. Keep thanking and appreciating your people.

Leaders have the foresight and ability to see the potential within people and then cultivate it into measurable growth

Never tell people how to do things. Tell them what to do and they will surprise you with their ingenuity.

and positive contribution. Leaders must keep strong faith in their people and help them flourish. Faith triggers hope in achieving something that is otherwise not possible by others. More than keeping faith, it is important to communicate faith. Great leaders like Mahatma Gandhi were able to stir the entire nation because of their ability to inspire faith and hope into the hearts of people. When people know that their leaders trust them, their motivation and productivity sky rockets. This way the followers enhance their self respect, which in turn brings them to respect their leader even more. When someone makes a mistake and accepts it, then restore the person because he already knows he has made a mistake. Explain to him his flaw, make him realise the gravity of the mistake and take corrective actions. Focus on intentions and not actions. Use positive communication to charge up the person who is anyways feeling low out of guilt. But it's very important to express that you know the mistake has happened. But as you know his fair intentions, so you should allow him to understand the reason on his own and check if he has understood it correct to avoid repeating the same. Create an environment where people do not fear failure, so

True leadership lies in guiding others to success. In ensuring that everyone is performing at their best, doing the work they are pledged to do and doing it well.

that people should not hide their failed attempts from you. They should be encouraged to speak about their failures and learn from them. People should be encouraged to take corrective actions. Create an environment where failures are discussed freely with examples and develop systems and processes to cut down the cause of failure. Once the whole team is empowered and made responsible, then they would come out with solutions and systems attacking the cause very effectively, and this way reduction in failures would take place automatically.

As a leader, seek first to understand, then to be understood. Avoid judging or concluding on a person. Give benefit of doubt to intentions and do not focus only on outcome apparently. Remove total fear at all levels, develop respect, show possibility of logical growth, treat people like your partners, learn to empathise, energise and empower. Trust me, the life will be far simpler, beautiful and worth enjoying.

THINKING BEYOND PERSONAL BENEFIT

Leadership is an opportunity to make a difference in someone's life, irrespective of the purpose.

People do not end up becoming leaders because of their capacity to envision alone, but it is the result of their capacity of "inclusive envisioning".

Until all of us have made it, none of us have made it.

Leadership begins with personal aspirations, goals and passion for growth. This is the stage when leaders have not necessarily assumed any leadership role or position. Once they are on their path of achievement of goals, growth becomes consistent and a new larger vision gets developed, which is vision beyond personal

"A good objective of leadership is to help those who are doing poorly to do well and to help those who are doing well to do even better."

—Jim Rohn

benefit. This is the time they start getting recognised as leaders and along with them they keep adding a lot of people who participate to achieve that larger vision. This vision normally goes even far beyond organisation or institution or community. A sense of empathy is developed with them and this elevates their vision to go beyond those who helped them in achieving their vision. Great leaders motivate large groups of individuals to improve the human condition.

No one is a born leader; people become leaders with the actions they take. If the vision is not large or inclusive in nature it would not attract people and a person will not be able to emerge as a successful leader even though he may achieve his temporary personal goal.

Leadership is about bringing people together.

This trait can always be best explained with the example of Mahatma Gandhi and Nelson Mandela whose vision was not only a national vision but it was for the whole humanity and generations to come. It was envisioning a thought or ideology which was missing or suppressed. However, I would like to explain this trait with the example of business leaders. People sometimes have a misconception that business leaders do not believe in inclusive growth. People fail to see the larger picture with the eyes of a businessman and hence, give rise to such a belief. According to me, even if you can employ one person and work honestly with him to achieve your goals, you are a leader who believes in inclusive growth.

The following example indicates that even when leaders think beyond their personal benefit, the size of the vision remains the same.

Bill Gates is the leader in Software Industry and Warren Buffett is the leader in the field of investment, each with net-worth of 53 and 47 billion USD respectively in March 2010. Now they are leaders in philanthropy through Gates Foundation endowment of 33.5 billion USD. Bill Gates is an American business magnate, philanthropist, and chairman of one of the biggest software companies, Microsoft. He is consistently ranked among the world's wealthiest people and was the wealthiest overall from 1995 to 2009, excluding 2008, when he was ranked third. Warren Edward Buffett is an American investor, industrialist and philanthropist. He is one of the most successful investors in the world. Often called the "legendary investor Warren Buffett", he is the primary shareholder, chairman and CEO of Berkshire Hathaway. He is consistently ranked among the world's wealthiest people.

Both these men have gone far beyond their professional/ corporate goals in individual capacity to achieve a much larger goal, which touches lives beyond their personal lives or lives of their shareholders.

The Bill & Melinda Gates Foundation, founded by Bill and Melinda Gates, is the world's largest private Foundation operating transparently. The most important aims of the Foundation are to enhance healthcare and reduce poverty, and in America, to expand educational opportunities and access to information technology. The Foundation is controlled by its three trustees Bill Gates, Melinda Gates and Warren Buffett with an endowment of 33.5 billion USD as of 31 December 2009. The scale of the Foundation and the way it seeks to apply business techniques to giving, makes it one of the leaders in the philanthrocapitalism revolutionising in global philanthropy.

On 15 June 2006, Gates announced his plans of transition out of a day-to-day role with Microsoft, effective 31 July 2008, so that he can devote more time working with the Foundation. In 2007, its founders were ranked as the second most generous philanthropists in America. Bill and Melinda Gates, along with the musician Bono, were named by the *Time* as Persons of the Year in 2005 for their charitable work.

On 25 June 2006, Warren Buffett, the then world's richest person, with estimated worth of 62 billion USD pledged to give the Foundation approximately 30 billion USD. Buffett's gift came with three conditions for the Gates Foundation: Bill or Melinda Gates must be alive and active in its administration; it must continue to qualify as a charity; and each year it must give away an amount equal to the previous year's Berkshire gift, plus another five percent of net assets.

Buffett gave the foundation two years to abide by the third requirement.

The Gates Foundation has become in a very short time a major influence upon global health. About 800 million USD that the Foundation gives every year for global health is equivalent to annual budget of the United Nations World Health Organisation (193 nations). This is comparable to the funds given to fight infectious disease by the United States Agency for International Development. The Foundation provided 17% (86 million USD) of the world budget for the attempted eradication of poliomyelitis (polio) in 2006. The foundation gave the Aeras Global TB Vaccine Foundation more than 280 million USD to develop and license an improved vaccine against tuberculosis for use in high burden countries. The Bill and Melinda Gates foundation has invested more than 250 million dollars in grants to create new small schools, reduce student-to-teacher ratios, and to divide up large high schools through the schools-within-a-school model.

An admiring announcement was made which revealed that Foundation would spend all of the Trust's resources within fifity years after Bill's and Melinda's deaths. This would close the Foundation. The plan to close the Foundation Trust is in contrast to most large charitable foundations. This has been done to lower administrative costs over the years of the Foundation Trust's life and ensure that the Foundation Trust does not fall into a situation where the vast majority of its expenditures are on administrative costs, including salaries, with only token amounts contributed to charitable causes.

If you look around, you would always see a gesture of inclusive growth and concerns, in decisions of every leader, which is beyond personal growth. All leaders possess this trait.

> *"Someone's sitting in the shade today because someone planted a tree a long time ago."*
>
> —*Warren Buffett*

INTEGRITY/HONESTY/ TRANSPARENCY

Integrity is a concept of consistency of vision, goals, values, principles, beliefs, expectations, methods, measures, actions, and outcomes.

Leadership is about winning without losing integrity in the process. The supreme quality of a leader is his integrity. Without it, no real success is possible, no matter whether it is in office or on cricket field or in army or in government.

Some traits of leadership like integrity can never be inherited or like materialistic wealth, they can never be transferred from generation to generation. In most of the cases, the heirs of so called leaders are not so successful. Many of the traits that a leader has, can be learnt, developed by following or copying them but the trait of integrity is most difficult to develop and copy. It can be developed if you are a true visionary working towards a larger goal of growth without being selfish about your personal growth. People tend to deviate from the path of integrity and tend to get indisciplined when their personal aspirations/goals/wishes take priority as compared to their larger vision of benefit for all.

Integrity is consistency and alignment of vision, goals, values, principles, beliefs, expectations, methods, measures, actions, and outcomes. Integrity is intuitive sense of honesty in regard to the motivations for one's actions.

The word "integrity" comes from the Latin adjective *intege,* which means whole or complete. It has more to do with inner sense of wholeness derived from qualities such as honesty and consistency of character. Integrity is the integration of outward actions and inner values. A person of integrity is the same inside as he is seen to the outside world. Since leadership is all about trust establishment, it is important not only to have integrity but also display integrity from time to time.

Integrity is display of sincerity, honesty, and candour in all actions. Deceptive behaviour does not inspire trust. No person can succeed without integrity. Even if one might succeed, the success would be temporary. Integrity is the core of every successful act. Whether dealing with staff, family, colleagues, or customers, one always wins if he has high level of integrity.

Getting 99 out of 100 in Integrity is same as getting 0 out of 100; It is either 0 or 100 there is nothing in-between.

Actually speaking there is nothing like level or degree of integrity. It is either 100% or nil. Without integrity one would never have followers because leadership is always about being a role model where people follow you, your goals, and success stories.

It is always easy to get your message accepted if you have high level of integrity. Let us accept the fact that every human being is smart and constantly analyses and judges people based on their moves, words, actions and thoughts. This entire phenomenon happens knowingly or unknowingly but it certainly happens. Whenever someone wavers on the grounds of integrity, he loses respect. One bad feature actually washes away all goods. Character matters and leadership descends from character. Leadership is a combination of strategy and character. If you must be without one, be without the strategy.

If you have integrity, nothing else matters. If you don't have integrity, nothing else matters.

"Nearly all men can stand adversity, but if you want to test a man's character, give him power."

—Abraham Lincoln

Integrity is the capacity to take fair decision in any situation. People normally remain fair when everything is going normal and positive but the moment the situation becomes tough or negative, probability to remain fair reduces. At times one becomes self centred and ends up taking biased decision.

Decision of a leader is always linked to a larger goal of life and an ultimate vision encompassing the overall interest of all involved. As a result of which, whatever decision a leader takes becomes naturally acceptable and is considered fair in the long run. At times the decision taken may not be popularly accepted but in the long run it normally turns out to be the best decision in the interest of the majority.

Clarity of thought, well defined purpose, well defined strategy and strong passion to achieve desired goals – all these together make every thought and action acceptable and believable. There is no room for lack of clarity, or doubt in the intention or lack of understanding in the actions. It kills short-sightedness and tendency to view immediate returns, as only long-term vision or far-sightedness prevails. Hence, by default, whatever they do, falls within the definition of integrity.

People at first don't follow worthy causes, they follow worthy leader; people buy the leader first then his vision.

Honest dealings, predictable reactions, well-controlled emotions, and an absence of tantrums or harsh outbursts are all signs of integrity. One litmus test of integrity is approachable behaviour. An honest person has nothing to hide, hence doesn't remain scared. He leads a very approachable and transparent life.

"In looking for people to hire, you look for three qualities: integrity, intelligence, and energy. And if they don't have the first, the other two will kill you."

—Warren Buffet

People want to follow an honest leader. When you assume a leadership position, you need to be clear that in the beginning people will always think you are a little dishonest.

One of the sobering characteristics of leadership is that leaders are judged to a greater degree than followers.

In order to be seen as an honest individual, you will have to go out of your way to display honesty. People will not assume you are honest simply because you have never been caught lying.

One of the most frequent places where leaders miss an opportunity to display honesty is in handling mistakes. Much of a leader's job is to try new things and refine the ideas that don't work. Opportunities to display honesty on a large scale may not happen every day. As a leader, showing people that you are honest even when it means admitting a mistake, displays a key trait that people are looking for in their leaders. By demonstrating honesty with yourself, with your organisation and others, you will increase your leadership influence. People will trust someone who actively displays honesty – someone who is worth following. Integrity is required to establish an ethical framework (both internally as well as externally) within the ecosystem.

What you set as an example will soon become the rule as unlike knowledge, ethical behaviour is learned more by observing than by listening. And in fast moving situations, examples become standards. Being a standard bearer creates trust and openness in the followers, who in turn fulfil the visions of a leader.

A leader being highly sensitive and observant is aware that he is being watched, analysed, and copied every second. As a process of evolution, we learn most of the things from each other and try to copy the same. It is very important for a leader to act in the manner he expects others to act. Whatever a leader thinks or whatever actions he takes, it gives way to a policy. They are viewed as role models in their organisation and hence, it is very important for them to do things in the right manner. That's how they set the ball rolling for standards. A leader is normally expected to be perfect.

Integrity is inspiring in nature. It radiates confidence in all actions. Integrity shows endurance – mental, physical, and spiritual stamina, which inspires others to reach for new heights. Man without integrity is like a cloud that brings no rains. If you lived in an arid land, imagine your disappointment when the dark clouds you saw and howling wind you felt actually brought no rain. Disappointment is same when the people fail to live up to their words.

If you tell the truth, you don't have to remember anything.

There is a connection between trust and integrity. Being honest is not enough, people need to be competent to earn our trust. To be a credible candidate for any job, a person needs skills and personal qualities to be effective in the role. Integrity is also broader than honesty. In addition to being honest, leaders with integrity must behave ethically. A criminal could be honest while breaking the law. Leaders with integrity must have an unwavering commitment to culturally accepted values and be willing to defend them. This requires them to do the right thing even if it is not in their personal interest. Leaders with integrity are responsible and consistent.

> *Leaders who win the respect of others*
> *are the ones who deliver more than they*
> *promise, not the ones who promise more*
> *than they can deliver.*

The best way to ensure the highest level of integrity is to:

- Be honest in personal and professional relationships.

- Be trustworthy and inspire trust in people around you.

- Be ethical and transparent in all interactions.

- Be fair, even when you compete and ensure all solutions have to be "always" win-win in nature without leaving any bad feeling.

- Be a thorough professional. Under commit but over deliver, without killing risk taking ability or creativity, or without tempting to keep undue buffer to your actual capacity.

- Be responsible for every action that you take.

- Be 100% punctual.

- Believe in quality in whatever you do, mind well, "whatever".

- Finally be CONSISTENT in all above.

I am again compelled to elucidate the trait of integrity through the example of Gandhi. Gandhi was a highly inspiring leader who displayed unshakable integrity in every action, thought and value. His life was simply a reflection of integrity. Gandhi's personal leadership capacity and power was highlighted by the fact that he accomplished his great mission to free India without any formal political, social or economic title or position. His life and work is a living witness that real power and influence comes from within, not from outside.

Through practise and effort, Gandhi developed integrity of character that few can claim. Albert Einstein said for Gandhi that "Generations to come will scarcely believe that such a one (Gandhi) as this walked the earth in flesh and blood". He dedicated his life to bringing his beliefs, thoughts, speech, and actions into integral harmony with truth.

When young, Gandhi went to England to study law. At times while alone he was pressured to eat meat which was against his religious beliefs. He was already married by then and his wife lived in India. He was offered temptations to stray and be unfaithful to his wife. He did not give in to any such pressure or temptations and stood firmly by his values, beliefs, standards, and convictions.

A woman once brought her child to Gandhi, asking him to advise her son not to eat sugar, because it was not good for his health. Gandhi replied, "I cannot tell him that. But you may bring him back in a month." The mother was upset as Gandhi moved on. She had travelled some distance, and had expected Gandhi to support her in her motive. She left for her home and returned later after a month as suggested by Gandhi but did not know what he would say. At that time Gandhi took her son's hands into his own, knelt before him, and tenderly communicated, "Do not eat sugar, my child. It is not good for you." Then he embraced him and returned the boy to his mother. The mother was grateful but confused to know why this could have not been done a month ago, so she asked, "Why didn't you say that a month ago?" "Well," said Gandhi, "a month ago, I was also eating sugar."

This was fascinating and it had cast a lasting impression. Gandhi's integrity was visible in every aspect of his life. He demonstrated integrity at the deep personal level making it simple enough for others to see and follow. His actions demonstrated that his internal commitments were authentic. He was real, without any mask. What Gandhi was for himself, what he was for others, what he wanted others to perceive for himself and what others perceived him to be was all same. There might be people who may not have agreed to his views or ideology but that was never a surprise to anyone. He displayed his ideology the way it was. It was the integrity of his character and the nobility of his courageous heart that won the respect of world leaders, admiration and support from millions of his countrymen in his quest to free India from British rule.

Such integrity has great power. This is what made millions trust him; learn from him and consider themselves as his followers. Collectively, they became a force strong enough to gain political independence for India from 300 year old British rule. True leaders demonstrate integrity by setting their own example.

Gandhi, though a practising Hindu, studied other religions such as Christianity, Islam, Buddhism, and understood the spiritual approaches to people believing in them. He developed the capacity to communicate effectively with members of other religions.

In the immediate aftermath of Hindu-Muslim religious riots that followed the partition of India, Gandhi went on a fast-unto-death if the riots did not end. After riots ended, a Hindu man came to meet Gandhi.He broke down before him and told him how he killed a small Muslim boy during riots because the Muslims killed his young son. Gandhi told him that though his actions can not be reversed but in order to expiate he must adopt a Muslim child of the age same as the age of his own son, who must have lost his parents in riots, and should be brought up as Muslim.

Gandhi knew something very precious even at that time, which most people still can not grasp with much ease. He knew that most of our apparent differences come from lack of unity as the starting point. Gandhi was able to inspire hundreds of thousands of Indians of varying faiths, religions, and castes to engage in acts of courage aligned with non-violence through integrity. People who supported Gandhi, knew that that they would be jailed and tortured but were undeterred because they supported truth and were bonded by integrity.

Integrity reflects the leader's ability to recognise and act upon the ethical dimensions of an issue. Great leaders display the ability to lift the question of ethics from that of the personal, and transform it into a question that reflects and impacts the ethics of all of humanity.

> "The things that will destroy us are: politics without principle; pleasure without conscience; wealth without work; knowledge without character; business without morality; science without humanity; and worship without sacrifice."
>
> —Mahatma Gandhi

SENSE OF URGENCY

Leader develops basic value systems, benchmarks and standards for his own performance; hence he starts viewing every activity with importance, links each activity with personal growth and takes each activity as support to the cause for which he exists. For him, there is nothing taken for granted and there is nothing like tomorrow. He would ideally love to execute tasks "yesterday" since each task is viewed as a benefit to his goal, vision, and is the very purpose for existence.

One of the tests of leadership is the ability to recognise a possible problematic situation before it becomes an emergency. Every leader who possesses a larger vision, strongly reflects this trait of sense of urgency. The reason why this trait is naturally developed in them is because they are very clear about what they want in life, there is clarity of purpose, and they can link every action with their larger goal. So they do not take anything for granted because they tend to see development in the achievement of end result in whatever they do. They normally execute only those actions which can be linked to their larger goals in life.

However while developing sense of urgency and executing certain tasks, one has to be little careful about timing and negotiations. Since sense of urgency should not be viewed as "need" by others, certain activities may be given some time to allow others to get involved and develop interest in it. Make sure that there is a thin line in this. So much time should not be given that the opportunity is lost. Leader's sensitivity to situations, strong analytical skills along with sense of urgency, leaves everyone involved impressed with the speed of delivery and quality performance. It is the sense of urgency which infuses speed in the actions through strong convincing skills in a leader.

Sense of urgency cannot be developed overnight. It is a gradual process. One has to take every single activity and every move with utmost importance. This particular trait enables a leader in analysing the details with speed and respond with urgency and accuracy, thereby making a timely move leading to timely solution, and efficient outcome.

Sense of urgency reduces the response time hence multiple decisions and actions can be taken in the given time frame. This increases the probability of right decision and saves resources.

A sense of urgency drives people, companies, institutions, and nations to work in a much efficient and productive manner. It makes people work as if their lives depend on it, which is actually true but seldom realised. Many a time we want to achieve so many goals in the long run but due to the impact of time we do not realise that every small action, reaction, and response helps in achieving the final long-term goal. This is as a result of our failure to link the impact of daily actions on long-term goals. Urgency is mainly related to crisis. We do not realise that if a situation is not handled immediately then any uncontrolled event may eventually result into full blown crisis whose consequences would always be adverse because of lack of planning and control.

In the book *The Road Ahead*, Bill Gates said that a secret to Microsoft success is they always think of themselves to be on the losing side, and this makes them strive to be number one every day. This attitude creates a sense of urgency which makes them work harder to survive in a highly competitive environment of IT industry.

As professionals, you suddenly experience a spurt in productivity and actions merely a day before final presentation of annual meet, or just before final meeting of merger, or a day before you plan to go on vacation. This primarily happens because we consider certain situations or events more important than others, and when we are close to those situations, we feel that there is less time and suddenly things start appearing urgent. There are so many activities happening around us that we are unable to segregate between urgent and important, and most of our activities end up becoming urgent due to delay. Whereas since a leader has the sense of urgency they do not waste time, and do not let a situation of crisis arise.

Once someone is trapped in the comfort zone, he loses the sense of urgency. He feels no reason to work hard and excel. He falls prey to the trap of mediocrity. Perhaps this is the reason why many family businesses don't succeed beyond the third or fourth generation. The younger generations are already in the comfort zone; they have lost the sense of urgency owned by the first generations. This also explains why many people do not grow, or grow slowly, in their life.

It is very important to understand that the sense of urgency automatically does not get created during crisis. Let us understand the process to inculcate the sense of urgency in order to enhance our productivity:

- Have a bigger vision and larger purpose in life...Clarity on what to achieve? A leader has vision. There is something BIG to pursue, which gives birth to a strong pulsating desire. A leader's vision is larger than life to be achieved in one life, which naturally develops sense of urgency. Without vision you have nothing to peruse, no desire to follow, no urgency, and hence very low productivity.

- Set challenging deadlines... By when to achieve? Vision of a leader is reflection of strong desire, which he wants to fulfil as soon as possible. So he normally lays down very clear timeline to achieve that, and try to reduce that timeline.

- Define process... Clarity on how to achieve? Due to leader's execution and integration capacity, he breaks vision into smaller goals and identifies actions for each goal, reintegrating them to synthesise a larger vision. Due to clarity of action, he is decisive in nature, hence able to act with urgency, and does not procrastinate. Most of the time people are not able to react despite wanting to react because they do not know the means, though may be clear on the end.

- Make yourself the owner of situation...Because a leader considers himself responsible, and accountable for the current situation as well as future outcomes, he also would consider himself responsible for failures, if outcomes are unexpected. Leaders can never digest unexpected outcomes. It is the feeling of winning that gives him satisfaction.

- Always be aware of the worst case scenario. Think multiple steps beyond next step. People normally do not think that far. They normally think only of immediate consequences of failure, and not about the rippling effect that one failure would have in future. It can result into multiple failures, creating a situation of full-fledged out of proportion uncontrollable crisis. Because of lack of ability to think several steps ahead, situations worsen, and crisis happens. Take example of Bhopal tragedy of Union Carbide or oil spill of BP in Gulf of Mexico. It is lack of urgency taking shape of a systemic pattern and converting into full-fledged crisis.

- Never give-up... People normally begin things or tasks with lot of enthusiasm, but after a few setbacks their enthusiasm fizzles out and they give up and lose on the sense of urgency.

As a leader, it is equally important to inculcate this character in the team too. By and large once a leader develops this; it normally percolates down if it is consciously communicated at every level. Not everyone would have a very large vision, but vision alignment with vision of leader would easily develop the sense of urgency with every other parameter in place.

As a leader, you can inculcate the sense of urgency in your team by the following steps:

- Clarify and simplify goals, roles, and responsibilities, and monitor the same with feedback. Each goal should be quantified with specific timeline. Never keep open-ended subjective goals. Keep communicating that again and again, and not only at the time of appraisals. Each person working in an organisation must be crystal clear on what is expected out of him in quantifiable form. Clarify the growth path. Define it as clearly as possible. Everyone should know that if they deliver with speed, they will grow exponentially, and land up in a very high position. Coach, counsel, and mentor proactively.

- Decentralise decision making as far as possible to encourage decision making at the bottom of the pyramid, because the symptoms of need for development of the sense of urgency are felt there first.

- Empower people to act and publicly praise urgent actions. When someone in your organisation—regardless of their level, moves quickly to make something happen, appreciate him and make sure everyone knows about it. Small acts of urgency have the power to inspire larger ones.

- Extreme enhancement of a two way communication. Design a well-crafted process of communication, percolating every thought to the bottom of the pyramid. It gets people energised and involved. Most of the time in presentations or in board rooms, talks of expansion, acquisitions, growth, and motivation remain restricted to top management, as a result of which monotony sets into the system at the bottom, killing the sense of urgency. Knowledge sharing creates the feeling of belongingness.

Message must incorporate deep rooted convictions of people whom you want to inform. Create a strong channel of information flow right from interpretation of vision to intermediate and short term goals. Channel of communication can be standardised in the form of internal newsletter of review meeting, or online portals, or letter from chairman, etc. Most organisations make the biggest mistake of opening up communication channels but only from top to bottom and not from bottom to top. It is very important to have an equally strong and efficient channel of formal as well as informal communication from bottom to top. This is crucial because in most crisis it is always found that someone at the bottom was in a position to sense the beginning of derailing of system but could not transmit the information to the top. Very simple example of this is when some key person who resigns which could have been avoided if the top management would have been aware of the step in advance. It is always later found that many people in the team were aware of the action he was likely to take. What stopped them from sharing this? Think! Would they have done the same if it was their own company? Kept quiet and let the crisis come or would have stopped the colleague from going to a competitor? That is why inculcate the feeling of ownership. Develop strong formal and informal channels of communication from bottom to top across divisions.

- Educate the team on consequences, both positive as well as negative. Share with the team best case scenario of suitable changes, and worst case scenario of lack of sense of urgency. Driving force through the leader has to be powerful enough to produce positive images of things to come that it excites people to bring the change. At the same time, also caution them with possible consequences of negligence or easy attitude, and how this can slowly but firmly take shape of a systemic crisis. Make sure that you do not get overboard into this, else instead of developing sense of urgency there may be a sense of fear or frustration in the team, despite nothing going wrong at the moment, because people normally like to avoid bad news so they may behave like an ostrich, and not listen and simply run away. If they resign, you may end up losing a good resource in an attempt to infuse the sense of urgency. Make sure while sharing this information, there should not be any feeling of building up of sense of pressure or fear in the team.

- Bring the team together. Convey optimism and passion. Think why soldiers fight on the border together without any personal benefit, for the nation, without fighting amongst each other. Create a benchmark. There has to be a goal to compete, or to fight against. It can be competing against a company, a system or whole industry, or it may be a global competition. Create a target and compete until you win. Develop spirit of competition. If you are already number one, then elevate the benchmarks or goals in terms of quality. Create larger goals. Make people busy. Create events. Infuse incentive schemes. Make the environment happening and teeming with activities. When this process is going on, there has to be a seamless flow of information, updating on growth, which would inject the feeling of winning. Celebrate the success beyond incentives.

- Re-engineer. It is important to keep infusing fresh energy into the system in terms of new initiatives, goals, people, training, etc., to make the system dynamic in nature. Go beyond sales and profit as parameters. Innovate better, newer, and more interesting ways of benchmarking and rewarding. Get your staff more interested in the industry by taking them to trade shows, by circulating trade publications, and talking about industry-wide news.

- Celebrate every success. Success motivates more success. Talk up how you're all on the winning team, and find every reason you can possibly think of to celebrate your success. Five years in business – celebrate! First million dollar month – celebrate! New product launch – celebrate!

While building "sense of urgency" in team from state of complacency or false urgency, one needs to observe and feel changes in the way people feel, behave, and act. Below table will help you develop your analytical capacity to sense the change in team.

> *"Sense of Urgency fuels the passion for purpose and electrifies the journey of execution of vision."*

	Complacency	False Urgency	Sense of Urgency
Wanted or Non-wanted	Not-wanted	Not-wanted	Wanted
Automatic or Consciously created?	Sets in unconsciously in the system over a period of time. Remains for longer periods.	Naturally gets built up in bad times. Doesn't last long.	Can never set-in automatically. It needs to be developed consciously by efforts. It is rare, important in a rapidly changing environment, and even in the absence of competition.
Cause	Monopolistic business. State of success or lack of competition for long periods.	Short-term sudden failures or disasters with long-term impacts creating fear across systems.	Leadership. People across hierarchy need to create it, especially when not needed, when things are going smooth.
How individuals think during this situation?	I know my job best and I am doing it. There is no better way.	It is a big mess.	Greater opportunities are everywhere. Let's identify one, and go for it.
How people feel?	Contented	Frustrated	Powerful pulsating desire to win.
How people behave/act?	Involved in monotonous activities as usual.	Fire-fighting and burnt-out.	Executing important focussed tasks with urgency. Actions reflect alertness, speed, confidence, continuity, and consciousness.

DECISIVENESS

Decision is always a reflection of your opportunity cost/next best alternative; people who fail to prioritise, fail to decide; there is nothing like right or wrong decision; take a decision and then make it right.

This trait is of unique importance. Without this trait any other trait is almost of no use. Reason and judgement are the qualities of a leader. Life is all about decision making. When we talk of decisiveness, one is "ability" to decide, and second is "willingness" to decide. It could be decision as small as choosing options from menu card in a restaurant when you go out on a dinner, or as big as selecting or rejecting a VP or CEO for your company in the interview; whatever the decision may be, it is important to take decisions. Success is just a decision away.

One of the reasons why leaders are able to take decisions is due to combination of the following factors:

- Clarity of vision. They know what they want, hence there is a strong desire triggered from within to achieve something, which creates a sense of urgency avoiding any delay in taking decisions.

> *Success is not a matter of chance; it's a matter of choice.*

- Clarity of means. How to get that is wanted? As a result of strong execution capacity and passion for purpose, they are ready to try multiple permutations and combinations to achieve what they want; hence they are clear not only on purpose but also on process. Many a time non clarity on "how" leads to confusion and may delay the decision.

- Clarity of timing. When to decide? Leaders always have a sense of urgency which pushes them to take a decision as soon as possible without any procrastination. Leaders normally do not make up because whatever they do is for themselves and not to please anyone else.

Leadership has a harder job to do than just choose sides. It must bring sides together.

- Integrating capacity. They are able to integrate the impact of current decision to what they want.

- Speed of thought. They have the ability to analyse pros and cons with speed, hence they are able to come to a conclusion much faster than an average person. This way they are able to

If you will make the decision, your subconscious will make the provision.

decide more quickly as compared to others. People often complain about lack of time when lack of decision is the main problem.

- Self-motivation. Self-motivation enhances their capacity to absorb failure, thereby reducing fear of failure. This automatically enhances their risk taking ability. Most of the time people do not take decision because they fear failure. What many people do not understand is that success is nothing but

If you don't decide to succeed then you have already decided to fail.

increased capacity to fail.

Decisiveness Matrix. Let us carry out an interesting exercise reflecting our decisiveness.

In the table below there are certain questions asked. Against each question you have to write either "Yes" or "No" based on the conditions explained. If the decision was taken by you, then write "Yes". If the decision was taken by someone else, then write "No". If the decision was taken by someone else and you agreed to that decision later, then write "No". If the decision was taken jointly, then write "No".

	In Life	This Year	This Month	Today
Are you clear on what you would like to do?				
Was this decided by you?				
Are you clear about the process, i.e. how to get about doing it?				
Was this decided by you?				
Did you know or do you know when to start doing?				
Was this decided by you?				
From where (place/ location) did you initiate or would you initiate doing it?				
Was this decided by you?				

Count total number of "Yes" and "No". Out of thirty two options, more the yes, higher is your decisiveness.

There would be some situations where it is important to delay the decision, in such situations do not misunderstand the leader to be indecisive. At such moments, he either prefers not to reveal the decision, or he has very clearly decided not to decide. This is not out of his lack of ability or willingness to decide but simply because he wants someone else to be decisive. In such situation, it is most important that the leader conveys his stand for not taking a decision because the team feels very helpless when the leader is not able to take a decision especially if they perceive him to be the decision maker, and even worst is when they perceive this as a result of his lack of willingness to take a decision without any concrete logic.

A leader's ability to take a fast decision is developed as an outcome of his overall nature. There are a couple of factors which play an important role in allowing the leader to take a decision:

- Being basically intelligent, their ability to understand the situations is too high so they understand a scenario quickly, and hence conclude intelligently with logic.

- Strong communication also adds to this. Many a time some people are able to decide but do not have skills to express their decision so they are unable to express in time.

- High sense of security and lack of fear of rejection. Many a time people are able to decide but they fear lack of acceptance of their decision by others, hence they do not execute. They may not be able to face the consequences as a result of non-acceptance or doubt their own capacity to reduce the adverse impact of the decision. In case of a leader's decision also, there may be resistance from certain groups of people, but his trusts on his capacity to reduce negative impact explains the logic and takes people along.

Lack of decisiveness has caused more failures than lack of intelligence or ability.

Decisive nature of a leader can best be explained by quoting some very important decisions taken by Winston Churchill. In July 1940, he ordered to attack French warships at Oran by opening fire at them. This decision was taken after the

French-German peace agreement in which it was agreed by France that warships would be handed over to the Nazis. Britain never wanted the warships to go to Nazis as it would strengthen German invasion fleet, which would be a potential threat to Britain. Britain offered France a proposal, to sink the boats, hand them over to the British Royal Navy or alternatively sail them to a neutral port for the duration of the war so that they be beyond the reach of Nazis. Britain affirmed that anything beyond these options, Royal Navy would be forced to attack, and attempt to sink or disable warships. Tragically, French commanders refused the British terms, and their warships were attacked. This attack resulted in killing about 1297 French servicemen. Churchill, found the decision tough but unavoidable. This tragedy on the other hand, however, sent a clear message that Britain was prepared to fight the tough way.

Another example of tough decision was Churchill's order that the wounded should be the last to be evacuated from the beaches of Dunkirk. At the time, the prevailing belief was that less than 50,000 could be safely evacuated and Britain desperately needed able-bodied soldiers for her defence. It, therefore, was undoubtedly a practical and strong call.

Most of the decisions we take are far simpler than the decisions we just saw, hence it's important to decide. Not taking a decision is sometimes even worse than taking a wrong decision. A life spent making mistakes is not only more honourable but more useful than a life spent doing nothing.

If you don't decide for yourself, someone else will.

EXECUTION CAPACITY

Vision, if not executed, remains a dream.

Leadership is the capacity to translate vision into reality. Leaders are not born; they are made through industrious effort and hard work. Leaders are not only good thinkers with good envisioning capacity, but they are equally good executors. Some people, who are good in thinking, fail to execute due to fear of failure. A leader is one who knows the way, takes up the way and then shows the way to others.

Because the vision that a leader follows, is his own brain child, he understands it the best. He can break that down into smaller goals. He takes up disciplined and intelligent measures with acute judgemental capacity to develop right actions to achieve each goal. Since he is involved at each stage, he can explain the situation best, even if these actions may be taken by people other than him.

If you want people to follow you, you have to know where you are going and how to get there.

Due to his strong communication skills, he is able to transmit his knowledge and understanding to others very clearly. He also develops tools to monitor each stage of progress. Thus, the overall execution is very well planned.

You can't lead anyone else further than you have gone yourself.

One more reason why he is able to get the tasks executed is the fact that he himself is a great executor. Leadership is never inherited; it is developed over a period of time by learning from scratch. Unless you learn to execute, you cannot become a leader. When we say learning to execute means developing the capacity to perform, it is not necessarily that we talk in terms of performing all small tasks ourselves. It is rather about knowing each detail of

It is not fair to ask of others what you are unwilling to do.

execution, even though it may be carried out by others.

There are so many actions that a leader alone cannot perform, but due to his clarity of vision, strong belief in his own vision, and perceived positive outcomes of the same, he is able to convince others in such a way that they align their vision with his. He also explains each of them the desired actions expected through them to get possible outcome, and provides them with tools and methods to execute.

You don't lead by pointing and telling people where to go. You lead by going there and making a case.

One simple explanation or reason for successful execution is nothing but "deep involvement". Whatever a leader does is not superficial; he is deeply involved in every activity, or has trained people who can get as deep as he can, in his absence. This is why he is the best executor.

There is nothing like leadership without execution; it is always leadership by execution. It is his clarity of execution that makes people convinced about his leadership and nullifies the necessity for him to execute every minute task. If a leader doesn't have an execution capacity, he would not be able to talk with ease and confidence, and thereby fail to convince people to carry out actions necessary for implementation and desired outcome. This is how he would fail as a leader.

Leaders go ahead and do something, others sit still and inquire, why wasn't it done the other way?

You can't monitor and audit every facet of your business/ activity, lest you won't have time to run the business. Execution matters most in monitoring the critical factors, what I call as "thumb rules". It is at these thumb rules, where execution can mean the difference between success and failure. A leader needs to focus as sharply as an eagle on thumb rules.

If we talk of any activity, be it manufacturing or service sector or even an NGO, there are always certain parameters which need to be identified. A leader should derive thumb rules for these parameters, and then set systems and processes to monitor if these thumb rules are achieved. Say, if we want to achieve top line and bottom line in banking business. One of the parameter to be monitored at the bottom of the pyramid is number of meetings done by marketing executive. Thumb rule set is, each person should be able to carry out, say, three meetings a day. Devise an online system whereby details of all meetings should be fed and the compiled report goes to branch manager. In every such business, there could be hundreds of such parameters and equal number of thumb rules depending on various scenarios. What leaders are good at is simplifying number of parameters to may be as low as seven to ten and identifying the right thumb rule for each parameter in that condition of business environment. Leaders are also good at identifying emerging parameters and deriving new thumb rules as per change in business environment. Most important is their ability to link thumb rules to a final measurable desired goal like profitability.

Leaders are problem solvers by talent and temperament, and also by choice. Leadership is solving problems. The day your team stop bringing you their problems is the day you have stopped leading them. They have either lost confidence that you can help them or concluded you do not care. Either case is a failure of leadership.

Thumb rules are true measurement of progress and success. These parameters are not sales or profits. Many people misunderstand and at times fail because they try to measure success by profitability or revenue. These are actually outcomes of success. By the time you know the outcome, it is too late to take corrective actions. Thumb rules help you decide whether you are moving towards the success or not, and if yes, whether your rate is enough to achieve success in desired time frame or not. Leaders are indeed excellent at dissecting the data and identifying patterns from that.

Thumb rules are those critical measurements which can be linked to quality of output, based on which an outsider forms an impression of you, deciding whether your offerings and their expectations are in alignment. Though they vary from industry to industry and business to business, every business has them. Understand them, identify them, define them, measure them, monitor them, and repeat this again and again until you achieve the desired output.

Leadership is about developing your abilities while discovering the abilities of others.

Execution doesn't mean staying busy, but knowing how to get the right things accomplished. Leaders know how to get people focussed on doing the right things that can make or break a company. They know that accepting no excuses from their team members means permitting no excuses from themselves as well.

Execution is everything. Dream all you can, plan all you want and then execute, else you have no right to dream or plan. Execution is what separates those with ideas from those with vision who eventually take actions to attain their goals. It is about strategising and implementing with power and conviction. Creating a culture of execution is the responsibility of leadership. It is all about getting things done in-time with consistency, efficiency and discipline; standardising systems and processes; and inculcating culture of ownership and accountability.

SENSE OF SECURITY/LACK OF FEAR

In the journey to fulfilment of vision, failure is far BEYOND success and not BEFORE success, hence a leader never fears smaller falls which at times look like failures to normal eyes that have sight but lack vision. He moves on the road to fulfilment of vision, taking everyone who comes along the way, sharing his vision, and sense of security which keeps oozing in the form of an aura or charisma making all equally convicted, and passionate about the journey.

All of us have different types of fear. The very genesis of fear is the fright of unknown. Fear is always of failure or loss of success. Fear is a word related to unknown outcome, or failure to achieve desired outcome, or loss of something already achieved. What we normally fear in any situation is unknown or unpredictable outcome. Leadership is a gradual process of overcoming fear of the unknown and developing a sense of security. Leaders are normally self-dependent people, it does not mean that they are loners and do everything by themselves, but they do not depend on any person or process or system or object to desire to achieve success.

A leader is a fanatic thinker, who can visualise the worst case scenario and normally prepares his mind to face the same. Being prepared for ultimate; intermediate scenario does not deter him. Sense of security is normally triggered by self-dependence. A leader is someone who wants to achieve something very big, but doesn't get affected on thinking of losing that, essentially because he has faith in his power to create from scratch. It is this attitude of leader which makes him fearless and develops a sense of security.

They tend to be free of guilt and have little or no need for approval. They are generally secure and free from guilt, and are usually unaffected by prior mistakes or failures.

Normally, fear holds normal people back from taking certain actions and they avoid trying new things in life. The less you attempt to do different things, the more you would end up doing monotonous tasks over and over again. As the world changes dynamically, doing the same thing that was working in the past, may not work anymore in the present, and certainly would become obsolete in future. Such people even fail to adapt to change. Leading the change, or causing change, or initiating change, is nowhere even in their distant thoughts.

A leader being a person with a high sense of security, automatically develops resistance to fear or goes in a state of neutrality, which enables him to try various things, allow him to experiment with his ideas and thoughts, and finally reach success after multiple unwanted or unpleasant outcomes.

Whenever a person achieves something, and becomes comfortable or content with that achievement, he develops a fear; a fear of losing what has been achieved. So he gets busier in protecting what is available. He is unaware of the fact that what led him to achieving something would not lead him to retaining the same because once you achieve something the dynamics change. Achievement is always in terms of relationships. You never achieve a designation or position, but you develop a relative respect in the eyes of others. You never achieve a personal relation in terms of making a friend or a life partner or a neighbour, but what you achieve is respect from that person. One must remember what actions led you to develop that respect from people in personal or professional relationship; the same actions won't work to grow that respect or maintain that respect because now the state/situation has changed and expectations change. People who did not know you, or were not connected to you before, were satisfied and expected little from you but now they know you, they are related to you, their expectations from you are more and you need to do more to satisfy them, and to retain their confidence in you. If a person doesn't grow or build his capacity, he cannot upkeep expectations, relations get diluted, jobs are lost, personal relations also break, and businesses collapse. All this happens because individuals do not want to grow. Once you grow at individual level, relations grow, expectations are fulfilled, and you are able to give and receive more at personal as well as professional level, hence getting a feeling of satisfaction.

Once people achieve something, they develop a comfort level, whereas in case of a leader, he always elevates his needs, and accordingly changes his methods, strategies, and tools to achieve the next level of comfort. Thereby, developing a higher level of respect from people around him, which comes in the form of higher designation, fulfilment, success, and more love from friends and family.

It is very important to give up fear of losing something or someone, once it is achieved; and at the same time it is equally important not to keep any fear in the process of achieving something, with anticipation of failure.

It is not that leaders are made of some special material that they are fearless. I have noticed that there is a certain degree of anxiety or fear *Information is the core of leadership.* in every individual, but leaders normally overcome this by information. Leaders are relatively more informed people. Fear is normally of the unknown. I have seen that when a leader decides to do something, he gets so much involved into that task, and digs deep, sucking possible available information on the topic that they update themselves of possible outcomes of various actions, hence reducing room for unanticipated outcome, thereby reducing fear. Another reason for lack of fear or sense of security is focus on "end" and not worrying on "means to end". A leader normally doesn't get trapped by outcomes of actions, but normally keeps the destination in mind while attempting various permutations and combinations of actions to achieve the desired goal. Hence, smaller failures don't bother him to give up attempts out of fear of non achievement.

Unlike others, a leader never hesitates to take action, because he is driven by a vision crafted with his own thoughts with highest level of conviction. In the process of deriving a vision, lot of information has been gathered,

---

analysed, and assimilated on that topic, which makes him most comfortable while building a road to success. The road may appear less travelled to others, but is thought of multiple times, and is being built in line with his thoughts.

As a leader, what to do, when to do, and how to do is decided by him, so, there is no question of unknown. Others fear unknown outcomes of their own actions because the actions are directed by someone else, so people who do not decide their own "whats" and "hows" always remain in the trap of unknown. For all those, who do not participate in the process of vision creation, their actions are like walking on the road blindfolded, directed by others.

Try to close your eyes and ask someone to direct you. You want to walk, but you do not know where to go, you do not even know how much to move, so the person who is directing you would guide you as per where he wants you to go and you will get what he wants you to get. Road will appear as wide as he says, and even if there is no obstacle, you would not run. Until you get something, you can just visualise through the direction of your guide. And even after you get that something, you can just feel and cannot see, hence the sense of achievement is much lower. Whereas if you decide what to do and how to do, you are doing things with eyes wide open, you can almost see most of the road, decide your speed, jump the obstacle, run on wide roads, and feel more satisfied on getting what you had seen and decided to get. There will almost be no chance of falling down, wasting time, injuring yourself, and most important, fearing something which anyways doesn't exist.

Many a time, I notice a lot of disappointment in people even after they complete the execution of tasks. Disappointment in people, most of the time when they get something what others had shown, is not because they were shown the wrong picture, but because they had interpreted something wrong.

Whereas, satisfaction in case of a leader is always more, because he gets what he had visualised and interpreted of his own vision.

Decide your own "Whats" and "Hows"; decide your own destiny, be a leader and you shall overcome every fear and immerse yourself in the sense of security.

Leaders do not feel sense of insecurity because they never seek security or comfort. Leaders are never driven by want of comfortable, non-risky, or secured environment. Leader's passion to achieve something large, drives him to put may things at stake, and that too multiple times. The magnanimity of the vision demands risk and insecurity by entering unexplored territory, so having decided to follow that vision, a leader has already given up the want of security and has mentally prepared himself for every kind of insecure or unknown situation which he might encounter in the process. Hence, the process of becoming a leader begins with giving up fear and attaining a sense of security from within, in any environment. Sense of security is not achieved after you take a leadership position, but first you attain sense of security and then the leadership follows.

A leader is always courageous, risk taking, calm, firm, and secured under any condition, which might appear insecure to others. A leader conditions his mind and prepares himself psychologically to feel highly secured much before he initiated the pursuit of his vision; else it is very difficult to initiate the very process of vision formation. What appear failures to others are already discounted upon by a leader. Say for example, Edison failed over 1,000 times before he discovered the formula for an electric bulb. But probably he had already conditioned himself to make more than 10,000 attempts before he could have given up, so he achieved his desired result with only 10% of the planned efforts. Leaders' capacity to attempt is so high that their definitions of failures are much different or just do not exist. Most of the time by the time they reach the so called failure, success is already achieved. Their definition of failure is beyond success and not before success.

> *Failure, to a leader, is beyond success and not before success.*

INTEGRATING

Role of a leader is like an orchestrator. He can sense the experience of synthesizing sounds of multiple musical instruments, which is difficult to visualise for musicians playing instruments of their respective expertise.

A leader can sense the strength of each person who comes in his life. He can integrate the strength of the whole team to create a powerful force, by synthesising each person in a strong relation, through his own relation with each of them. Leader integrates information, people and situations.

Basic process in envisioning by leader is nothing but information integration. There is lot of information available to all of us in different forms and mediums at different times. A leader integrates the pieces of information available and creates something meaningful, which others fail to understand, until integrated by him. He has different perspective on things. Once he integrates the available information and understands the present scenario, he visualises and predicts likely changes in the future and identifies an opportunity in the process. He at times triggers that change. He creates a vision, breaks down the vision into minute understandable, achievable and non-integrated goals. While he allocates the tasks to achieve these goals, back of his mind he initiates the process of reintegration. When each goal, is being achieved simultaneously, or in sequential order depending on the resources available, the leader is busy identifying and reintegrating. When people begin to understand the larger picture, the organisation has already moved into a different orbit.

Most important part in team building is integration of people. Leader is an integrator of relations. He carries along people with varied interest, nature and capacity, by binding them together through a common goal. He has immense capacity of expectation management in order to ensure that the integration remains intact. Speed of each person is totally driven by him, depending on the resources available to achieve the outcomes. When resources are available, you see everyone charged with energy in execution to achieve higher output and create a buffer of resources for the worst times. When resources are scarce, you still see people around a leader charged with energy in team formation, training, gathering knowledge, and similar activities related to preparing for maximum output in best times without drifting away in frustration out of slowdown in speed of execution. In the absence of leadership, such situation creates a sense of fear and drop of confidence within the team. A leader can integrate people with almost "conscious hypnotism" like situation.

A leader understands demand supply so well that he can identify the resources in vicinity of demand, link it to the cost of supply and integrate the resource mobility for desired production in most scientific fashion. This gives maximum, most economically viable and quality output. This principle applies to every type of activity and not just to a business activity.

More the information he gets, more he spreads his capacity to integrate, ultimately attaining a global position. If you observe a local leader, he manages to integrate locally available resources to fulfil local demand, whereas if you analyse an international leader, he integrates the resources available throughout the world, and meets the global demand, making best use of the resources available internationally. Depending on the leader's capacity to gather information, he decides the size of his vision, thereby synthesising and integrating all the information and resources available in the fulfilment of his vision.

Leadership means integration of information, people, and situations.

CHILD-LIKE CURIOSITY TO LEARN

Leadership and learning are indispensable to each other. Curiosity is one of the permanent and certain characteristics of a vigorous mind.

Have you ever observed a child in the first two years after birth? You can see several strong senses a child develops, and that too without any "formal training"! They cultivate a sense of recognition, learn to drink, eat, smile, cry, speak, and demand. He learns a language to the extent of understanding and expressing basic needs. Even without understanding the language we speak, he can sense to differentiate between family members and outsiders. Have we ever thought why and how this happens? As a human we are blessed with the capacity to "learn on our own". This learning continues till we die. We learn simply by observing. It is most essential here to understand that we would anyways learn what we want to learn, and if we are not interested in something then despite a lot of training we would never learn. There were never any formal classes required to use any email, or mobile phone, or social networking site. Whether you are young, or old, your capacity to learn remains the same; what changes is your curiosity to learn. As we grow old, our curiosity to know things subsides, we develop tendency to believe to have attained some kind of expertise on certain topics. This doesn't happen as a child because we are open to information; we do not believe ourselves to be an expert and do not stop allowing information to flow through us. As we grow, we start comparing. It is important to compete, but useless to compare. It is most dangerous to learn to conclude on our judgements. You must learn to analyse and judge, but do not conclude or decide, without experiencing or giving a chance to a person or situation.

I often wonder if as a child, one has the capacity to learn the whole language without any formal training, or expert intervention. If so, then why do people need formal training on soft skills when they join a profession? Companies need to spend a lot of money to train matured individuals the basics about how to talk or how to approach, the so called soft skills training. Why we cannot learn by observing? Why there is a drop in learning capacity of the same person after such a rich experience of spending so many years talking to people? Why there is no formal training on how to behave at home with parents or wife? Why there is a formal training on how to talk to a customer? Is it not as basic as how to talk to a human being? Were we taught on how to cry if we are hungry soon after birth till we learn to speak? Were we given training that this is how one 'smiles', and you should stretch your lips by few centimetres or sometimes even millimetres and others would feel good? Were we trained as a child that when we go in a garden to play, we should mingle with kids? Why then we need to take session on business etiquettes on how to exchange cards in a business meet? After spending years on this earth talking all the way, we surprisingly spend money on training to speak!

As we grow, we lose on "child-like curiosity" to know things, to observe, to learn. We need an environment to learn as we grow, but as a child we learnt almost everything in any environment just by observing and experiencing things. If you observe a leader, he always maintains that child-like curiosity to learn things. He does not require any push from outside, or any right environment. Every situation is right for a leader to learn. Leaders challenge themselves and push themselves to grow.

Sometimes questions are more important than answers. Judge a man by his questions rather than by his answers.

Whenever we talk to kids, and if they do not understand something, we would be flooded with why, what, how, explain, I didn't get you, so on and so forth. When we are in school or say college, the tendency to ask questions goes down. As we grow older, when we start our professional careers, we further lose on our curiosity and question even lesser. Many a time during presentations we need to probe with questions like "'I hope you have understood?" or "could you please elaborate on what we just discussed?" It is at that time we come to know that what was just said was not understood, but still no question was asked. What could be the reason for such behaviour? Reason is the loss of curiosity to learn, fear of how others might take it if we ask. We are more concerned of how others would feel rather than what we understand.

As we grow old we learn to conclude and not try further. Our habit of concluding on situations, people, and systems without going in depth reduces our scope of learning. It is very important to keep analysing, taking views, and judging though not concluding. Your senses may say that the person doesn't seem to be helpful, but do not conclude and stop approaching; you never know when things click and your long pending task is done in just a few seconds. Do not hesitate to ask or demand. Many a time we wait for the right time before we approach someone, but trust me, there is no right or wrong time. Often decisions taken by people are random. Keep asking, approaching, and attempting; in some cases it clicks, in some it won't but do not lose on your curiosity to know more and learn more.

Leaders always have that curiosity to learn on the topic of their choice. They are fully engaged into that and learn as much as they can from every possible source coming around them. In order to keep the learning alive, most important habit one should develop is habit of reading books. Decide a topic of your interest, pick up a book and just let yourself flow with the thoughts of the writer. It is important to understand that when someone writes a book, he is at his best, and tries to share his knowledge in the best possible manner on that topic. It is always good to read biographies of successful people. Make it a compulsive habit to read a biography at least thirty minutes a day. I am sure you would be much more evolved than what you are otherwise. Invest in books, create a mini library at home, share books with friends, gift books, take membership of a library, gift your child/friend/spouse a library membership, and most important, share knowledge.

> *"It is miracle that curiosity survives formal education"*
>
> *"The important thing is not to stop questioning. Curiosity has its own reason for existing. One cannot help but be in awe when he contemplates the mysteries of eternity, of life, of the marvellous structure of reality. It is enough if one tries merely to comprehend a little of this mystery every day. Never lose a holy curiosity.*
>
> *—Albert Einstein"*

EMOTIONAL/PSYCHOLOGICAL MATURITY

Leader possesses highest level of sensitivity to interpret others' expression of emotions, and express his own "desired" emotions, irrespective of the situation, in the best interest of the final goal, the purpose, and the vision...

In the process of evolution as a human, there are certain processes that we go through in terms of gaining maturity. It includes physical maturity, intellectual maturity, emotional or psychological maturity, and spiritual maturity. Apart from physical maturity, which is mainly genetic in nature and to some extent can also be built; other maturities depend on external environment and our efforts to change the external environment. It's a two-way process.

Emotional maturity is an internal development of balancing the mind and intellect with the external reality. It is nothing but the process of overcoming emotions and getting close to reality. It is a process of moving in to zero emotion and 100% reality.

We all have twenty-four hours in a day to perform our tasks. Life is about 1% what happens to us and 99% how we respond to things. As humans we have certain needs/ requirements. Our response to anything that happens to us is in context with these needs. Leaders though have capacity to envision large and desire to achieve big, they do not necessarily react in the context of the desire in their mind. They do not, let what they want come in the way of how they should react to a fact. Emotional maturity is the quality of our response to a situation. In a situation, a matured leader looks for facts. Once the facts are found, whether we accept them or not depends on the maturity of the mind. Leader has the capacity to quickly move close to the facts and start working out possible solutions to convert the situation in his favour.

Let us understand why a leader possesses emotional maturity:

- Clarity of purpose of life: A leader is very clear about his vision, what he wants; so anything that doesn't affect his vision, anyways doesn't bother him. If a situation positively affects his goals, he lets it happen. If a situation negatively affects his goals, then he quickly gets into action in the process of fact finding with a calm mind and makes best use of the facts to take a decision without any personal ego, or any other emotion coming his way purely in the interest of his vision/goal/purpose of life.

- Sense of urgency: Sense of urgency also plays a big role in this. When a person is emotionally affected, he ends up wasting a lot of time playing around his own emotions. A leader normally is not a person without emotions, but has the capacity to quickly overcome emotions by understanding facts. Sense of urgency doesn't allow him to ponder over issues through a glass of emotions. He is highly practical and thoroughly professional in his behaviour.

- Decisiveness: Decisiveness allows a leader to quickly act, by deciding the next step and then moving on. People become emotional when they are not able to decide the next best alternative. A leader being decisive in nature is always aware of his opportunity costs and jumps to the next best alternative rather than being indecisive and making his present an extension of the past.

- Thinking big: Degree of being emotionally mature is directly proportional to your capacity to think big. A leader's vision is so large that the outcome of any particular event, be it positive or negative, is never large enough to distort his larger picture. Hence anything doesn't emotionally affect him much. This also includes emotional impact of positive outcomes. They never become too excited, or sad, because like every other event, this too would pass, and one needs to move on in the pursuit of goal, which keeps getting elevated and larger.

- Leaders are normally highly intelligent people, so

calculating and evaluating the right situation doesn't take much time for them.

- They have high level of sensitivity to understand and feel others emotionally.

A leader keeps facts in mind and uses emotions to positively influence people. When a plane is hijacked, or a public place is under attack, or when there is natural calamity, a leader doesn't react with panic but stays calm. He quickly gets into action to bring back normalcy by ensuring proper allocation of available resources to counter negative impact. Most importantly, he always shows positive emotions to restore faith of people and prevents ripple effects of a negative event. He articulates a picture of "situation under control", thereby helping in the damage control process.

A leader with emotional maturity takes into account the situation, circumstances and all the facts. He is able to manage a tough situation since he sees what is happening and can extrapolate to what worse can happen if this situation continues. He is very clear that any emotional expression – likes or dislikes, anger or attachment, fascination or frustration – cannot change the facts. If we do not hold on to the facts, emotions overpower us. Emotions also sometimes influence matured leaders but they come out of it quickly since their focus is on the facts and solutions rather than problems. In any situation, the misperceptions caused by emotions are unveiled by a leader and he is able to see the reality more clearly to determine the correct course of actions.

A study has found that, of all emotional signals, smiles are most contagious and they have irresistible power to make the other person smile in return. The greater a leader's skill at transmitting positive emotions, more forcefully the enthusiasm is transmitted. With that kind of talent they become emotional magnets.

Emotionally matured leaders have the stamina to resist emotions and stay calm in stressful situations. Their behaviours are non-impulsive and they resist temptation to inappropriate involvements. They are capable of finding acceptable outlets for emotions. They understand conflicting views of others and express their opinion based on facts with openness and concern for overall effect.

In order to understand the process of emotional maturity, we need to understand how people react emotionally at various stages – under normal to extreme positive as well as negative situations.

- People, who are highly emotional, normally lose control. Even on a very small success they throw a mega party costing as much as the profit from that success. Or, at a very small failure they feel emotionally so weak, sending signal of failure across the team. Negative vibes spread like fire in jungle. It becomes a leader's job to quench the fire by positive emotions. It cannot be over by even being neutral in that situation. One's emotions interfere with work effectiveness. Frustration and negative emotions are expressed inappropriately. Emotional break out and incorrect personal involvement with subordinates, peers, or customers is visible in this level of extreme emotional immaturity.

- Next higher level of emotional maturity is when someone avoids stress by staying away from situations that provoke negative emotions. This is the state of being neutral. It is not a state of being close to the facts, but it is a state where even facts are avoided. This is the state of avoidance. Stay away from situation as well as facts.

- Next level is facing the situation, but resisting the temptation to engage in incorrect emotional involvement, or impulsive, behaviour. Fact finding still doesn't start.

- At the next level, the person uses methods of emotional control to prevent burnout, or over-enthusiasm. This way he deals with ongoing emotions effectively. A leader responds constructively at this level where he controls strong emotions and takes action to respond constructively to the source of the problems.

- Next and the highest level is where a leader not only resists naturally negative or positive emotion, as a reaction to a situation, but finds facts and develops more constructive emotion which can add value to the purpose or goal. Here, the person not only controls the likely emotions but also develops emotions, which can positively influence and push others around him to act in the favour of faster achievement of the goal. It not only helps in the case of negative situations when a person stays calm and declares situation under control and allows the fighting spirit to remain alive; but sometimes too much of positive reaction also slows down the team in the anticipation of success, which is actually much more distant than perceived. So here, a leader also remains calm, tones down his positive emotions, thereby declaring the team to go on. This is a stage beyond controlling his natural emotion to developing a desired emotion, and thereby infusing desired emotion in others and controlling emotions of others. This process can be very much visible in the stage-shows of good singers. When Michael Jackson cried his fans not only cried but also fainted. A leader has the capacity to charge people around them with desired emotions.

Leadership is a matter of having people look up to you and gain confidence, seeing how you react. If you're in control, they're in control.

Emotion is like an energy, which can be transferred from one person to another and can also be amplified. A leader knows how to control this energy within him and transcend this energy into others, and control their emotions by controlling his own emotions. Once a frequency or a wavelength with people around him is set, then their emotions would simply move in tune with that of the leader. This can be done by simply understanding the basic needs of people, like the need for affection, security, creative expression, recognition, new experiences, and self-esteem; and by genuinely trying to help people overcome negative emotions and infuse positive emotions for the collective betterment and movement towards the final goal.

> *Leadership is about making others do what they don't want to do, to achieve what they want to achieve.*

CONCLUSION

Conclusion

As we reach the end of this book, I would like to end it with the intention of giving all my dear readers a new beginning. The traits discussed in the book are a glimpse of my observations and understanding of how leading results in sustainable growth and how the spirit of achievement keeps us energised and makes us infuse others with energy. How the capacity to gracefully lead attracts more people to be part of that energy in motion is what I have put forward for you through my experience-based writing.

I'm sure many of you will get charged and feel motivated after reading this book. However, some of you may also differ with what I have stated in these pages. My only success in writing this book lies in making my readers charged with energy and enthusiasm to lead and win in their life. Make sure that this feeling never gets fizzled out. The master key that I have given you in the form of this book will help you to keep the leadership spirit alive. Just read and refer to these pages again and again, and infuse certain practises in your daily routine to make your life successful. The process will get systemised by falling in deep love with yourself and by developing passion for growth, by holding strong belief in every single decision you take and by sticking to it until you win. Nothing would happen overnight; you'll have to put in constant efforts to accomplish your goals.

As you will nurture a large vision after getting inspired from this book, one most important thing to be kept in mind is never to expect that people will buy your vision as it is. There would be many who would not be in agreement with you. Take care to respect them as much as you may respect the person who is in agreement with you. Listen to all. Do not look down upon any one, even those who cannot perform as per your expectations.

Life is all about decision making and relationships. Never consider any decision to be right or wrong. Just believe in yourself and take the decision that suits you the most and be insane enough to make it right. Make sure while you are in the process of achieving what you desire, welcome those who participate in that and at the same time respect those who do not agree with you. Someone who is not in agreement today may agree tomorrow, and someone who is with you today, may decide to part with you tomorrow, and may again be part of your vision at some later stage in life. So, adopt the manner of remaining calm; thank those who are with you, who were with you and also those who are not with you because they may be with you in the future.

You may decide to part with someone, but make sure you do that "with respect". Learn to part amicably. No school or college or any degree course teaches how to relieve someone from team or how to resign. Learn to disassociate, or say "no" with dignity for others and respect for them. If you are a group leader and you decide to remove a person from the group due to whatever reason, make sure you do not insult him. Rather express your disagreement with genuine respect for that person. Make sure even after the person gets disassociated with you, he should never be against you. Similarly when you are part of a group and you decide to move out of that due to whatsoever reason, do not give surprises. Talk to the leader, share your views and see if there can be any possible solution or alternative. Before finding an option outside the team/group/company, talk openly about your expectations and disagreements. You never know things may materialise and you end up growing together. It is a process of goal/vision alignment and team building.

In 90% of the cases, I have seen when people communicate their disagreements openly with genuine respect for each other; they end up on some common ground and end up continuing being with each other. Genuine respect for each other is something that is very vital. Do not make opinions about any one, do not conclude, because people change, situations change, you change, and so do priorities. Always keep doors for opportunity open. Let positivity flow from all directions.

Once you start leading in the true sense, you would start humbling down; you would respect everyone's views, and opinions, and naturally most people would start following you.

Dream real big and lead to witness the entire universe working in your favour for your growth. Enjoy every bit of your growth.

Last but not the least, I would like to thank all my readers and request them to share this copy with family, friends, acquaintances and colleagues, so as to circulate the message of importance of leading and winning. Let us all be leaders in our respective fields and let all of us teem with prosperity and happiness. I want my readers to be leaders. I wish you all a successful life!

Desire is the starting point of all achievements,

identify your starting point;

let the journey of success begin!

www.ingramcontent.com/pod-product-compliance
Lightning Source LLC
Chambersburg PA
CBHW070509200326
41519CB00013B/2756